CONCEPTS OF TEACHING:
PHILOSOPHICAL ESSAYS

Edited by C. J. B. MACMILLAN
and THOMAS W. NELSON

RAND McNALLY & COMPANY · Chicago

CONTENTS

PREFACE

If there is any task upon which philosophers of education agree they should work, it is the analysis and explication of pedagogical concepts, the concepts that are used whenever a teacher or parent or other educator begins to discuss what he is doing. And if there are any central pedagogical concepts, they are the concepts of teaching and learning. This book is a collection of recent papers concerned with the first of these.

One need not, of course, limit oneself to recent philosophical literature for intricate and interesting analyses of the concept of teaching. In many of his dialogues Plato raised significant questions about the concept of teaching, and practically every philosopher since then has been concerned with the concept of teaching or at least has made passing remarks about teaching. But only recently has a special literature begun to form around this concept. This is partly the result of the analytic training of many modern philosophers of education and partly the result of the recent emphasis in empirical educational research on the problem of describing accurately and fruitfully what goes on when someone teaches another.

There are many conceptual problems and practical issues associated with the concept of teaching. A full discussion would require covering such varied areas as social institutions, human nature, value theory, the nature of knowledge and, indeed, all of the problems of philosophy, psychology, and social science. Merely touching on all these would require a mammoth tome. This more austere volume focuses on two concerns: the first five papers are concerned in one way or another with the logical relations between the concepts of teaching and learning. Chapters six through eight are concerned with the pattern of reasoning involved in teaching or implied by the concept of teaching. Among these eight papers, of course, there is a great deal of overlap—questions raised in the first chapter are touched on in all that follow.

We have collected these papers from their widely scattered sources because we have found them useful both in introducing our elementary students in philosophy of education to this crucial concept and in extending the vision of our more advanced students. The first group can too easily get bogged down in the overwhelming complexity of educational issues if they do not have specific arguments and concerns to discuss. The latter group needs to consider in great detail the concerns and contradictions that underlie these analyses and the type of argument found in them.

But there are other audiences for these papers as well. General philosophers may be interested in the discussion of questions which were first raised by Plato; practical educators of all sorts (whether involved in educational institutions or merely concerned with teaching their own children) will find some nourishing crumbs here; educational researchers and policy makers could find clarity where all too often confusion reigns. Although the collection was designed for our own convenience, it should be helpful to all these and to others who are just interested in philosophical discussions.

Special debts of gratitude are owed to our colleagues in philosophy of education at Temple University: Robert H. Holtzman, James E. McClellan, and B. Paul Komisar. Their interest in the problems associated with the concept of teaching has sparked our own interest, and their suggestions for this collection have been of inestimable value.

Philadelphia   C. J. B. M.
May 1968   T. W. N.

CONCEPTS OF TEACHING:
PHILOSOPHICAL ESSAYS

B. Paul Komisar and Thomas W. Nelson
Temple University

I. INTRODUCTION:
CONCEPTUAL ANALYSIS OF TEACHING

In the time just passed, research on teaching was dominated by small-group studies on teacher leadership styles. Groups of students, pasteurized to remove contaminating variables, were exposed to different modes or styles of teaching, and the experimenter catalogued the results for the different student populations. This design was supposed to discover the superiority of some methods of teaching over others for the groups tested. What it tended to produce instead was a discouragingly lengthening list of contaminating variables, which, when isolated and taken into account in grouping students for further research, made the experimental situation more and more unlike the actual classroom. This approach to studying large complexes of variables is just now fading, though its potential viability faded some time ago.

Most of the present research on teaching remains empirical in that it continues to study descriptively what happens in the process—particularly the verbal process—of teaching. But the aim now is to generate taxonomies for counting and codifying the variety of behaviors teachers engage in when they teach. Such research, under a charitable interpretation, belongs to the 'science of education.' Unlike the studies on teacher leadership styles, however, it tends to be nonexperimental.

In sharp contrast with these two 'scientific' approaches to studying teaching is the small movement that tries to get clear what is or might be *meant* when we speak of someone as teaching something. It is one thing to report (classify, count) what teachers *do* when they are in the classroom and quite another to say how we know that what they are doing is rightly *called* teaching. Put yet differently: What is the cor-

A major revision of "Conceptual Analysis of Teaching" by B. Paul Komisar in *The High School Journal* 50: 1 (October 1966) pp. 14-21.

rect (or a defensible) concept of teaching? And given such a concept, what denotations fall under it? These questions are the central concern of the first half of this volume. What we seek to discover is the meaning of the *term* teaching—not facts about how teaching is or might be conducted.

It remains an unsettled issue what single name should be applied to this kind of study. "Analysis of concepts," "elucidation of meaning," and "conceptual mapping" are all likely, though perhaps inexact, attempts at characterization. But baptism would not change the activity, so we propose to use any and all of these as (or if) the impulse for variety becomes irresistible.

What is it we seek to produce through the analysis of the concept of teaching? This is a more serious question for us. We cannot say straightforwardly that we seek to describe the concept of teaching because of the phenomenon in educational circles of what might be called the 'bloated concept of concept.' Unfortunately, in most educational jargon a concept of something (e.g., readiness or education) includes not only a statement of the meaning of the term (readiness, education), but also bits of facts, anecdotes (sometimes called 'theories'), and even value judgments regarding the actual phenomena. Thus, according to the bloated view, the *concept* of readiness would encompass, among other things, the fact that tests are devised to measure it, that it is a state of precondition for something, and even that teachers should pay attention to its presence or absence in learners. Construed in this way, a concept of anything would sequester a good portion of all the information we would want to cite in a complete elucidation of that phenomenon. Unfortunately, nothing we discuss in this study is likely to quench this often premature thirst for total knowledge.

The quick way to avoid the excesses of the bloated concept is to assert boldly that a conceptual analysis of teaching should culminate in a definition of the term teaching. This may be too sparse a statement to accurately describe our purposes, but an error in the direction of austerity in any educational context at least refreshes. To overcome whatever difficulties attend this severe limitation of the scope of the analysis, we have but to be benevolent in setting out criteria for what is to count as a definition. Specifically, there are two difficulties to be overcome:

1. The task of defining the term teaching is too easily read as filling in the end of the formula X means Y. We do want things to be more

complicated than this, for even though we can find explanatory synonyms for X, they are not likely to be both informative and exhaustive. Thus, a term like instruction seems an adequate substitute for teaching, much of the time. Yet it seems appropriate also to consider whether teaching might not on occasion take place in the absence of instruction, so that the analogy is imperfect as well as uninformative. A synonym is obviously not what we seek as a definition, for even if we could find a linguistic substitute for teaching, we can still ask why either term is applicable to the situation. Our venture has to do with finding and delineating the conditions under which the term is applicable.

2. The second difficulty with the limited statement of purpose is that it may foster the mistaken belief that a complete definition of teaching is already at hand. The truth is that for technical purposes we have no adequate definition of teaching. In behavioral science, it is often assumed that a specified operational definition of a term like teaching can easily suffice for testing a particular educational hypothesis. In a sense this is true, but one always runs the risk of challenge: Teaching as operationally defined may have nothing to do with teaching as we ordinarily understand it.

To sum up: It is silly to think that anything as simple as 'teaching means instruction' will do as an adequate concept elucidation. And even the most exhaustive of presently available definitions does not begin to satisfy even preliminary requirements for completeness and accuracy. Consider the following as an illustration of how even the best of present definitions remains unsatisfying. (In addition, the discussion of why and where the definition went wrong will give us a chance to show some of the criteria that a definition must satisfy.)

> By teaching, we mean, for the present purpose of defining research on teaching, any interpersonal influence aimed at changing the ways in which other persons can or will behave. The restriction to "interpersonal" influence is intended to rule out physical (e.g., mechanical), physiological, or economic ways of influencing another's behavior, such as pushing him, drugging him, or depriving him of a job. Rather, the influence has to impinge on the other person through his perceptual and cognitive processes, i.e., through his ways of getting meaning out of the objects and events that his senses make him aware of.
>
> The behavior producing the influence on another person may be 'frozen' (so to speak) in the form of printed material, film, or the program of a teaching machine, but it is considered behavior nonetheless. How the

other person "can or will behave" refers to his capabilities for maximum performance, i.e., his abilities, or to his modes of typical performance, i.e., habits or attitudes, that constitute the objectives of instruction. The behaviors and intervening variables mediating them (such as abilities, habits, or attitudes) may be classified in many ways, such as the "cognitive", "affective", and "psychomotor" domains of the *Taxonomy of Educational Objectives* (Bloom, *et al.*, 1956).[1]

We repeat that we consider this one of the better specimens. Notice that we are given a lengthy elucidation of teaching and not merely directed to a few 'clarifying remarks.' All the same, taken as an attempt to report the meaning of the concept teaching, it is open to some objections.

The definition quite plausibly classifies teaching as a form of influence on "the performance potential of others" (thus suggesting that teaching aspires to something more than changing behavior). Further, in this definition an attempt has been made to distinguish teaching from activities that influence dispositions of others, but are yet not teaching. More technically, several points need to be made:

(a) Only some—the more remote—of the related activities are considered explicitly; the definition tries to demarcate teaching from drugging or excluding from employment by making *interpersonal influence* a defining criterion of teaching. Such a distinction does seem to exclude physical, psysiological, and economic influences of one person on another, true—but it does not succeed in setting off teaching from all other activities. Indeed, we doubt that it works smoothly to exclude even the other activities cited; for giving drugs and firing people are just as personal (or impersonal) as informing another or sending someone to the library or assigning homework. (Even application of force, such as pushing, may be part of a very personally influencing lesson on the limits of freedom.) If these are not forms of interpersonal influence, then it appears that interpersonal has become a very technical term, itself in want of definition.

We are tempted to suppose that the defining criterion here should have been *verbal* interpersonal influence (dialogue, etc.) rather than simply interpersonal influence. But the fact that such an issue arises should remind us that something is unclear about the definition. And if there is anything which such a definition should do, it is to clarify the term defined, not uncover further ambiguities. *Interpersonal* seems to cause more problems than it cures.

---

[1] N. L. Gage, "Paradigms for Research on Teaching," *Handbook of Research on Teaching*, ed. Gage, (Chicago: Rand McNally, 1963), 96 f.

(b) A second and more serious matter needs to be dealt with. The illustrative definition includes some elaboration on the criterion of interpersonal influence: the influence must work through perceptual and cognitive processes. That is, to be a case of *teaching*, an activity must influence people through the medium of ideas, meanings, etc. It is difficult to be sure whether this new point is supposed to be consistent with, qualifies, or replaces the term interpersonal influence, but the addition is welcome. What we find wanting in the definition, thus far, is attention to other 'influencing' activities that are considerably more likely to be confused with teaching than drugging. The crux in the business of defining is the necessity that teaching be distinguished from, or be shown to overlap with, such activities as indoctrinating, advising, and the like. How does the definition we have been considering meet such a test? Not well. It will not do to say that teaching involves cognitive abilities, because so do related activities. It is clear that one can influence the performance potential of another through cognitive operations and yet not be teaching. The point of the difference between teaching and indoctrination, for example, is *how* or to what *end* we engage the cognitive factors. Not *that* we do so. (Of course we can read "cognitive ability" another way to make it more restrictive. But making the restrictive sense clear is what the game of definition is supposed to be about.)

(c) There is another important point to be made with respect to interpersonal influence. Consider the following question: Can there be no interpersonal influence and yet be teaching? On the definition given the answer must be no. Yet patently the answer is yes. That is, if we construe influence to mean (at least in part) *producing* a change of some sort, notably learning. It is obvious, however, that teaching can exist where there is no success at producing learning. This is only to say that there is an *intent* as well as a *success* use of the term teaching. But this point ought not to be pushed here, for the definition speaks of "influence aimed at changing." This seems to separate influencing and changing, which would vitiate this objection (though not forestall another about the meaning of influence).

(d) Finally, one might ask whether, after all, the term influence is not too strong a word to employ as a defining characteristic of teaching. Influence, in the accepted sense not revoked here, would seem to have affinities with *making* something happen or *producing* changes. Of course all these interpretations are compatible with a scientific model of teaching. (Gage says the definition is meant for a "research on teaching" context.) But it is still questionable whether teaching should be conceived as an activity that effects changes in students, or as one that simply affects students in certain ways. Influence is a perfectly good term to describe teaching and is as neutral as interaction, *if and only if the various qualifications noted above are all made*. But without these added restrictions the term influence carries with it unjustified connotations; it seems to favor a stronger model of cause and effect for teaching than present evidence confirms, so that the definition, which was to be reportive, has taken on a clearly persuasive aspect.

This is enough to expose our task. The purpose in investigating this sample definition, we remind you, was not to issue gratuitous criticism of one of the better attempts at characterizing teaching. Our purpose was to choose a definition attractive and rich enough to illustrate: (1) the sort of definition being sought in the present volume, and (2) some criteria by which such definitions are to be assessed. Since the objective is to produce a definition that reports rather than reforms our common understanding of the meaning of teaching, this study seeks criteria for usage which, when applied, result in uses of the term which are in accord with those we ordinarily recognize as correct. Hence we test the defining characteristics of the term by finding whether they include examples we all admit are instances of teaching and exclude cases we recognize as nonteaching, such as propagandizing or preaching. This was the procedure followed with the illustrative definition. We questioned, for example, whether the defining characteristics could be complete or accurate when the definition failed to distinguish teaching from such closely related activities as indoctrination. We also tested our defining criteria by determining whether they allow or disallow proper inferences to be made with respect to our commonly held concept of teaching (if a definition of teaching posits that teaching must *always produce* learning in students, for example, then it is wrong; in our common understanding of teaching, no such implication holds).

There is more to be said about the requirements that may properly be imposed on our search for a definition, but this will come later. It is sufficient to note now that the criteria we find may be numerous and intricately related. Certainly we may also in the end sum them up in a tidy defining formula: X means Y. But even if such a move is possible it will be the very least of our moves.

Now for an important qualification. In addition to reporting common usages, definitions function in several other ways (and it must be noted that our illustrative definition may have one of these other functions). Rather than report the common meaning of a concept, we sometimes *recommend new meanings* for terms through the medium of definition; we often use a definition to announce our decision (henceforth) to use a term in a special way. (These separate functions of recommending or legislating new meanings for terms are often assimilated under the single label "stipulated definition.") Definition can also function as a provisional setting of a subject matter as a preliminary to studying it. In making such definition, we may not aim at completeness or intend it to be used as a precise instrument; it may be sufficient to impose very crude limits on a phenomenon in order to specify them more precisely at a later time. Indeed, in terms of reportive accuracy a definition of this kind simply may be wrong. Its value is heuristic; it aims to satisfy psychologically the researcher that he has a hold, however slight, on his subject and to stimulate further research. Many definitions of teaching are of this sort, including our illustration, no doubt. For these it may not be important that they sharply set off teaching from cousined activities like counseling. The researcher may not wish to offer an exclusive definition at all. Instead he may merely wish to examine some crude property found both in teaching and in some related activities. He may speak of a study of teaching simply as a convenience, to alert us to the general sort of activity at which he happens to be looking.

When definitions are employed in any of the services discussed above, it is idle to criticize them for lack of scope or precision. However this may be, there is a very subtle distinction to be made at this point. Often, something like the following can happen: Arbuthnot does very much want to study, talk about, or do research on teaching—and not some other activity. We look at Arbuthnot's definition, however, and find it discouragingly deficient. Yet all the same, we begin to feel satisfied that it is indeed teaching he is studying. How can we account for this? We can account for it easily by borrowing the common distinction between using a term correctly and describing how the term is used. Arbuthnot is able to recognize instances of teaching with the best, but he is hopeless when it comes to telling us why they are instances of teaching.

This is why we often settle for demonstrable error in definition even in the most rigorous discussions of the subject of teaching. It is not purity or rigor or any other quality in the definition that disarms us; rather it is our sound intuition (or trained perception, if you prefer) in recognizing teaching. That is, we are masters of denotation even while we are inept at articulating connotation. This has to be true, else how could we ever test our attempts at stating the meaning of a concept? So we begin this study assuming that we all know (most) acts of teaching when we see them. But here we have the aim of getting clear on why (on what account) we can be so confident in our recognition. We cannot be sanguine about our chances for success, but perhaps we will at least find a path leading to the edge of the wood.

This search for a definition can be done at leisure. But patience may not be a virtue in regard to another quest. Let us introduce this issue by returning to yet another point in the illustrative definition. We refer to the explicit inclusion of films, machines, and such among the items the definition is said to cover. This listing is apropos, for it is precisely when new cultural forms that are like and yet unlike the well-labeled old forms arise, that we pause to study those words grown stale with custom. So it is with 'teaching.'

Two changes are in the making which give timeliness to the ancient activity of analysis of educational concepts. One is the introduction of new devices for the teacher which are not to be assimilated without consideration of why there should be any change at all. Another change, much associated with gadgetry, is the return to policies of education which would require more self-direction of the learner by engaging him directly in tasks without the intervention of a teacher. This, we suggest, is the natural moment for analysis of the concept of teaching. For these changes, and the issues they force, are not simply matters of changing the direction of effort of an otherwise internally untouched institution. These are the deeper changes that require us not only to reorient our policies of pedagogy, but also to recalibrate our pedagogical concepts.

We make this hasty point as a way of hinting at a premature answer to the question: What is the function of conceptual analysis? (Or Why do we want a complete definition of teaching?) The question is presumptuous of course. Read in a certain way, it is absurd, too. Not every intellectual activity must be accompanied by a full and well advertised report of its services. All the same, the question is there and wants answering. The best answer would no doubt consist in a recital of the many *specific* obscurities and perplexities from which analysis can or does deliver us. For it can be granted immediately that analysis has most to do with mistakes about words, and its service is usually polemic.

There is not space enough or time to embark on a fresh discussion of unhappy examples of talk about teaching. Especially so since we will need more equipment than an introductory chapter can supply. Discussion of all these items will have to come later.

But this is a congenial circumstance to react generally to a point of view that frequently gives rise to questions about the value of conceptual discussion generally. Inveterately, the person who asks such a question (in a mocking tone) is a victim of what we might call the 'empiricist-practicalist' ideology. According to this ideology, the only significant 'intellectual' work (as opposed to practical work, such as teaching, administering, etc.) is experimental testing of refined hypotheses. Moreover, detailed advice about curricula and conduct of schooling is construed as a paradigm of obviously profitable information. Naturally, elucidation of concepts is fairly remote from the activities favored under this approach.

But here it is the perspective on the activity that does us disservice, not its performance. For the position explicated above is a myth and one of the costlier iniquities foisted on us by the empiricist-practicalist ideology. History tells us a different story of the significance of conceptual analysis. The cycles of educational change have nearly always begun with a new conceptual orientation in which general maxims of educational practice are inextricably embedded. And it is these changing conceptual systems that direct shifts in educational policy, even as they prompt the empirical research that is voluminously and tiresomely cited as justifying the policy shifts. But the joke is that even in these early stages, the research is more promise than achievement. And as the research advances, the original principles are found unclear and inconclusive: research findings become ever more tentative and our understanding less sure. Meanwhile, the greater the uncertainty regarding the original principles, the more they are refined and qualified to save the face of truth, the more intense is our dependence on them to buttress the daily changes in education. Should the research trail be hacked deeper and deeper into unexplored territory, an ever widening gap will develop between the researcher who, increasingly doubtful that anything is to be found in this direction, slackens his pace and the schoolman who, unable to imagine any other direction to take, lengthens his stride confidently.

But at this point (or often even before skepticism and despair emerge) the whole conceptual set is replaced when another conceptual flaw is uncovered; yet another research effort begins; again educators announce new changes of policy based on these new 'findings of science and research.'

Surely there is a lesson in this familiar story. It is that a fertile seed-bed for educational endeavor lies in general conceptual systems. Refined empirical research *and* practical policies of schooling are *both* independent yet simultaneous outcomes of changes in educational concepts, which yield educational change by reorienting it. Empirical research has not been known to change education significantly by concretely advising it. We do not even begin to understand how to conduct a cumulative, ideologically neutral science of education; nor do we have even the slightest apprehension of rational means to practical decision making in education. (Both would free those activities from being directed by changes in conceptual systems.)

We are not making the silly suggestion that analysis is the answer to these woes (if they are woes), but analysis is certainly relevant—in a claiming race of also-rans, anything with legs stands out. And conceptual analysis is the only entry that shows much promise.

B. Othanel Smith
University of Illinois

II. A CONCEPT OF TEACHING

It is well understood that words can be defined to satisfy the purpose
of the individual who uses them. For this reason many controversies
center in the meaning of terms. The literature of education is filled
with claims and counter-claims about the meaning of "education."
One authority defines education as growth; another says it is the cultivation of intellectual virtues; and still another claims that education
is the means by which civilization is transmitted from one generation
to another. These definitions are controversial because each one is
packed with a set of preferences about what is to be taught, how it is
to be taught, who is to be educated, and so on. And conducting the
controversy consists in unpacking the definitions, each side pointing
out what the opposing view commits us to, what it denies or fails to
include, and at the same time claiming its own conception to be more
defensible and desirable.

The word "teaching" is used in various ways also, and definitions of
it often lead to or underlie controversial discussions in pedagogical
circles. While the unpacking of various definitions of "teaching"
would be an interesting undertaking, it is not our purpose to do so in
this article. We shall attempt to undercut conventional definitions by
developing a descriptive rather than a normative concept of teaching
and to distinguish it from other concepts with which it is often confused.

Reprinted from *The Teachers College Record*, vol. 61 (Feb. 1960), pp. 229-232. The
analysis reported here was made pursuant to a contract with the United States Office of
Education, Department of Health, Education, and Welfare.

DEFINITIONS OF TEACHING

Three uses of the word "teaching" are found in ordinary discourse. First, it is used to refer to that which is taught, as a doctrine or body of knowledge. In the expression "the teachings of the church" reference is made to a body of ideas or a system of beliefs. Second, "teaching" is used to refer to an occupation or a profession—the profession of one who instructs or educates. Finally, "teaching" is used to refer to ways of making something known to others, usually in the routine of a school.

We are concerned here with the third of these uses and shall disregard the first two altogether. "Teaching" in this third sense has been defined in the following ways:

Teaching: arrangement and manipulation of a situation in which there are gaps or obstructions which an individual will seek to overcome and from which he will learn in the course of doing so.[1]

Teaching: intimate contact between a more mature personality and a less mature one which is designed to further the education of the latter.[2]

Teaching: impartation of knowledge to an individual by another in a school.[3]

From a generic standpoint, each of these definitions suffers from the same defect. It smuggles in its own particular view of how teaching is to be carried on. All are question-begging definitions, for they answer in advance the very question which research on teaching seeks to answer. The first of these definitions commits us to the view that the individual learns by engaging in problem solving, and that he is motivated to learn by involvement in an unsettled state of affairs for which he has no ready-made response. To teach is to engage and direct the pupil in problem solving. Once we accept this definition, we commit ourselves to a chain of propositions identified with a particular theory of education.

The second definition just as surely, though perhaps less obviously,

---

[1] Adapted from John Brubacher, *Modern Philosophies of Education* (New York: McGraw-Hill Book Company, Inc., 1939), p. 108.

[2] Henry C. Morrison, *Basic Principles of Education* (Boston: Houghton Mifflin Company, 1934), p. 41.

[3] Adapted from common usage.

incorporates a theory of didactics. Teaching, we are told, consists in contacts between two individuals, one more mature than the other. The contacts are to be intimate and designed to advance the education of the less mature person. Education, by this definition, is the development of the individual through learning, and learning in turn is defined as an adaptive process. Intimate contact supposedly requires the presence of one person in the company of the other. To unpack this definition of teaching would again bring to view a theory of education.

We are no better off when we turn to the last of these three concepts. The definition of teaching as the impartation of knowledge is typically used by persons who think of education as the cultivation of the mind, the mind being thought of as an accumulation of information—factual, theoretical, and practical. Teaching, according to this definition, typically takes on the character of lecturing.

To say that the foregoing definitions are question begging is to say that teaching is confused with didactics. The way in which teaching is or can be performed is mistaken for teaching itself. In its generic sense, teaching is a system of actions intended to induce learning. So defined, teaching is everywhere the same, irrespective of the cultural context in which it occurs. But these actions may be performed differently from culture to culture or from one individual to another within the same culture, depending upon the state of knowledge about teaching and the teacher's pedagogical knowledge and skill. Didactics, or the science and art of teaching, are not the same as the actions which they treat. A definition of teaching as such, which packs a set of biases about how these actions are to be conducted, confuses teaching with its science and its art.

TEACHING AND LEARNING DISTINGUISHED

Furthermore, teaching is frequently assimilated to learning. The belief that teaching necessarily entails learning is widely held, and is expressed in more than one book on pedagogical method. As one of our most distinguished authorities says, unless the child learns the teacher has not taught.[4] Then he goes ahead to say that teaching is to learning as selling is to buying, apparently on the assumption that if there is no buying, there can have been no selling. At first, this binding of

---

[4] William H. Kilpatrick, *Foundations of Method* (New York: Macmillan, 1926), p. 268. See also John Dewey, *How We Think* (rev. ed.; New York: D. C. Heath & Company, 1934), pp. 35 f.

teaching and learning together after the fashion of selling and buying seems plausible enough. But the analogy will not bear inspection, although it does highlight the responsibility of the teacher and the importance of active endeavor by the pupil.

To begin examination of the idea that teaching entails learning, let us note first of all that teaching and selling each involve some sort of interaction. We do, perform, or accomplish many acts unaided. We race, hunt, and sing without the assistance of anyone. But there are actions which can be performed only in association with other persons. We can do business only if there is somebody to do business with. We can negotiate if there is someone to carry on negotiations with, and not otherwise. Likewise we can carry on the activities of selling only if there is someone who will buy our product and we can teach only if there is somebody whom we may instruct. Were there no buyers, there could be no sellers. Unless there were pupils, there could be no teachers. Such verbs as "negotiate," "sell," and "teach" signify proceedings between two or more individuals, involving some sort of deliberation with adjustment of mutual claims and interests in expectation that some result will issue. Lacking a process of interaction there can be neither teacher nor pupil just as there can be neither seller nor buyer.

Beyond this point, the analogy between teaching and selling begins to break down. To see how this is so, let us spell out the analogy. There are four elements in the selling-buying operation: a seller, a buyer, the act of selling, and the act of buying. Similarly, in the teaching-learning combination we find a teacher, a pupil, the action of teaching, and the activities of learning. To say that a teacher is to teaching as a seller is to selling, while not strictly correct, does not do violence to either of these relations. The qualifying expression "not strictly correct" is inserted because there are several different actions which we expect of a teacher: making assignments, grading papers, showing how to do something, telling why something is the case, and so on. But there is little more than one sort of behavior predictable from the statement that one is a seller (not a salesman); namely, that he gives something in return for a consideration, usually money. Looking further we find that learning is not co-ordinate with buying, because the relation of pupil to learning is not the same sort of thing as buyer to buying. We can say that a buyer is to buying as a pupil is to "pupiling," but the parallel breaks down when we say "as a pupil is to learning." "Pupiling," if there were such a word, would be required by the analogy to mean receiving instruction just as "buying" means receiving something in return for an agreed-upon price. Nor are we any better off if we substitute "learner" for "pupil," since "learner" is defined as one who receives instruction.

Furthermore, the relation between selling and buying is not the same as that between teaching and learning. The statement "I am selling X and someone is buying it from me" is implicitly tautological. It is clear from common usage that in order to be selling something someone must be buying. It would be contradictory to say "I am selling X but no one is buying it,"[5] or to say "I am buying X from so and so but he is not selling it." If you state "I am selling X" you are stating only part of what you mean, for implicit in this statement is the idea that someone is buying it. On the other hand, "I am teaching X (meaning, say, mathematics) to A and he is learning it" is not tautological. It is not contradictory to say "I am teaching X to A but he is not learning it." Nor is it contradictory to assert "A is learning X but no one is teaching it to him." "I taught X to A" means that I showed A how to do X, or told him such and such about X. This expression does not include the idea that A learned from me how to do X. It is thus not repeating the idea to add it to the expression. Hence "I taught X to A" says something different from "I taught X to A and he learned X." However, the parallel suggested in the paragraph above is logically similar to that between buying and selling. To assert "I am teaching X (mathematics) and he is 'pupiling' it" (meaning he is receiving my instruction) would be tautological. It would then be contradictory to say "I am teaching X (mathematics) and he is not 'pupiling' it" (meaning he is not receiving my instruction). To give instruction would seem to entail receiving it. It would likewise be contradictory to say "he received instruction, but no one gave him instruction."

The difference between teaching and learning may be further explored by reference to the distinction which Ryle makes between what he calls task words and achievement or success words.[6] Task words are those which express activities such as "racing," "treating," "traveling," and "hunting." The corresponding achievement words are

---

[5] There is a sense in which it would not be contradictory to say "I am selling X but no one is buying it." For example, "I have been selling cars all day but nobody bought one" is not self-contradictory. But in this case it would be more precise to say "I have been trying to sell cars," etc., meaning "I have been doing things intended to result in the sale of cars."

[6] Gilbert Ryle, *The Concept of Mind* (London: Hutchinson & Company, Ltd., 1952), pp. 149-52.

"win," "cure," "arrive," and "find." *Teaching* is a task word and *learn* is the parallel achievement word. Achievement words signify occurrences or episodes. Thus one wins, arrives, or finds at a particular moment, or a cure is effected at a particular time. Nevertheless, some achievement verbs express a continued process. A boat is launched at a particular instant but it is held at the dock for inspection. On the other hand, task verbs always signify some sort of activity or extended proceedings. We can say of a task such as play, treat, or teach that it is performed skillfully, carefully, successfully, or ineffectively. We may play the game successfully or unsuccessfully, but we cannot win unsuccessfully. We may treat a patient skillfully or unskillfully, but the restoring of health is neither skillful nor unskillful. It makes sense to say that we teach unsuccessfully. But it is self-contradictory to say we learned French unsuccessfully.

Israel Scheffler
Harvard University

III. THE CONCEPT OF TEACHING

A. RESTRICTIONS OF MANNER

Every culture, we may say, normally gets newborn members to behave according to its norms, however these are specified, and many cultures have agencies devoted to this job. But not every way of getting someone to behave according to some norm is teaching. Some such ways are purely informal and indirect, operating largely by association and contact, as languages are normally learned. But not every formal and deliberate way is teaching, either. Behavior may be effectively brought into accord with norms through threats, hypnosis, bribery, drugs, lies, suggestion, and open force. Teaching may, to be sure, proceed by various methods, but some ways of getting people to do things are excluded from the standard range of the term 'teaching.' To teach, in the standard sense, is at some points at least to submit oneself to the understanding and independent judgment of the pupil, to his demand for reasons, to his sense of what constitutes an adequate explanation. To teach someone that such and such is the case is not merely to try to get him to believe it: deception, for example, is not a method or a mode of teaching. Teaching involves further that, if we try to get the student to believe that such and such is the case, we try also to get him to believe it for reasons that, within the limits of his capacity to grasp, are *our* reasons. Teaching, in this way, requires us to reveal our reasons to the student and, by so doing, to submit them to his evaluation and criticism.

From Scheffler, Israel, *The Language of Education*, 1960. Courtesy of Charles C Thomas, Publisher, Springfield, Illinois.

17

To teach someone, not that such and such is the case, but rather *how* to do something, normally involves showing him how (by description or example) and not merely setting up conditions under which he will, in fact, be likely to learn how. To throw a child into the river is not, in itself, to teach him how to swim; to send one's daughter to dancing school is not, in itself, to teach her how to dance. Even to teach someone *to* do something (rather than how to do it) is not simply to try to get him to do it; it is also to make accessible to him, at some stage, our reasons and purposes in getting him to do it. To teach is thus, in the standard use of the term, to acknowledge the 'reason' of the pupil, i.e. his demand for and judgment of reasons, even though such demands are not uniformly appropriate at every phase of the teaching interval.

The distinctions here discussed between teaching and fostering the acquisition of modes of behavior or belief are, we may say, distinctions of *manner*. They depend on the manner in which such acquisition is fostered. The organic metaphor, as we have seen, focuses on the continuity of the culture's life,—in effect, on the behavioral norms and beliefs forming the *content* of the culture. It makes no distinctions in manner of acquisition of this content, of the sort we have illustrated by referring to the concept of 'teaching.' It is these distinctions, however, that are central to moral issues concerning social and educational policy. The usefulness of the organic metaphor in certain contexts cannot be taken to show that the distinctions of manner referred to are of no practical or moral moment, that, for example, teachers ought, by any means and above all, to adjust students to the prevailing culture (specified in any way you like) and to ensure its continuity (no matter how specified). Whether teachers ought or ought not to do just that or some alternative is an independent and serious moral question that requires explicit attention. That it receives no emphasis in the organic metaphor indicates not that the question is unimportant, but that this metaphor is inappropriate in practical contexts.

We shall end this discussion by trying to show how fundamental the question of manner is, and we shall refer here again to the concept of 'teaching.' We have already taken pains to indicate that the notion of teaching is considerably narrower than that of acculturation. The fact that every culture may be said to renew itself by getting newborn members to behave according to its norms emphatically does not mean that such renewal is everywhere a product of teaching in the standard sense we have discussed. To favor the widest diffusion of teaching as a mode and as a model of cultural renewal is, in fact, a significant social option of a fundamental kind, involving the widest possible extension of reasoned criticism to the culture itself.

That this option may, in particular societies, lead to great changes in fundamental norms, beliefs, and social institutions, with respect to the prevailing culture, is indeed possible, even highly likely. But such a consequence need not always follow. In particular, it is not likely to follow where the culture itself institutionalizes reasoned procedures in its basic spheres, where it welcomes the exercise of criticism and judgment, where, that is to say, it is democratic culture in the strongest sense. To support the widest diffusion of teaching as a model of cultural renewal is, in effect, to support something peculiarly consonant with the democratization of culture and something that poses a threat to cultures whose basic social norms are institutionally protected from criticism. Such support is thus consistent with the vision of a culture where understanding is not limited and where critical judgment of policy is not the institutionalized privilege of one class, where policy change is not perforce arbitrary and violent, but channelled through institutions operating by reasoned persuasion and freely given consent. Many, even most, social thinkers have shrunk before such a vision and argued that culture cannot long survive under democracy in this sense. Others have urged the fullest institutionalization of reasoned criticism, fully aware that such a course indeed threatens societies with rigid power divisions, but denying that all societies are therefore threatened and that *no* culture can survive which rests on free criticism freely interchanged. The issue, in short, is not whether culture shall be renewed, but in what *manner* such renewal is to be institutionalized. It is this fundamental practice issue that must not be obscured in practical contexts by metaphors appropriate elsewhere.

B. TEACHING

We have . . . indicated how the notion 'teaching' suggests a crucial distinction with regard to the manner in which learning may proceed. What was involved in this phase of our discussion was, of course, the everyday, standard use of 'teaching,' and not some stipulated use. This standard use deserves further, detailed attention, for the word figures centrally in numerous discussions of education where the context makes plain that it is to be taken in the ordinary way. We turn then . . . to an examination of the term 'teaching,' in an effort to understand the ways in which it is typically applied, and that to which it typically refers. Our concern . . . is thus to provide an account of the accepted meaning of the notion 'teaching.' We shall not, however, attempt to provide here an explicit definition, but only an informal discussion of certain elements of this accepted meaning.

We may begin by recalling the difference . . . between "success" and "intentional" uses of the verb 'to teach.' In the "success" use, a word refers to more than just the doing of something; it refers also to the successful outcome of what one is doing or has done. To have built a house is more than to have been occupied in building activity; it is also to have gained success in this activity. So, to have taught someone how to swim is more than to have been occupied in teaching someone to swim; it is also to have succeeded.

Let us now, for the sake of simplifying the process of our analysis, abstract from considerations relating to success, and restrict our inquiry to "intentional" uses of the verb. With such a restriction understood, we may classify the teaching referred to by the verb as an activity: it is something that one normally engages in or is occupied in doing. Jones may be engaged in teaching Smith how to operate an electric saw, just as he may be engaged in painting his house. Indeed, to say of Jones that he is teaching is normally to convey that he is engaged in teaching.[27] Teaching is, further, directed toward a certain result: it is a goal-oriented activity.

It is worth noting that not everything true of Jones and expressible by a verb form can be so described. Jones is not normally said to be engaged in breathing, sitting, or strolling, though he breathes, sits, and strolls. Though he owns property, he is not said to be engaged in owning property; although he has reached the age of 57, he is not ordinarily described as having been occupied in reaching the age of

---

[27] This matter of what is normally conveyed or understood by a statement concerns something weaker than what is implied by the statement. Nowell-Smith has discussed such a notion under the label of "contextual implication." See P. H. Nowell-Smith, *Ethics* (London: Penguin Books, Ltd., 1954), p. 80. He writes, "I shall say that a statement *p* contextually implies a statement *q* if anyone who knew the normal conventions of the language would be entitled to infer *q* from *p* in the context in which they occur." He also stresses that contextual implications may be expressly withdrawn, but that unless they are withdrawn, we are entitled to presume that the inference holds in the context in question. The notion of what is normally conveyed though not implied by a given statement need not, of course, be interpreted just in the way Nowell-Smith interprets it; the present text uses the notion but is neutral with respect to variant explanations of it. For other recent analyses of teaching, see B. O. Smith, "On the Anatomy of Teaching," *Journal of Teacher Education* (December 1956), 7:339 and "A Concept of Teaching," *Teachers College Record* (February 1960), 61:229.

57. Teaching is engaged in, it is directed toward a goal the attainment of which normally involves attention and effort, and provides a relevant definition of success. Breathing, sitting and strolling are not oriented toward goals in specifiable ways; we do not speak of success in breathing, sitting, or strolling. To own property and to reach the age of 57 do not embody strivings for certain goals; they are not even described as things being done. "What is he doing?" may be answered by "He is sitting," ". . . is strolling," ". . . is hunting," ". . . is teaching," but not by "He is owning property," ". . . is reaching the age of 57." In the latter cases, indeed, the present participle is normally inapplicable altogether. We may say "He owns," but not "He is owning"; we may say "He has reached the age of 57," but not ". . . is reaching the age of 57."

By contrast, if Jones is working on a puzzle, he is trying to solve it; if he is said to be painting his house, he is normally understood to be trying to get it painted; if he is described as teaching Smith how to operate an electric saw, he is normally taken to be trying to get Smith to learn its operation. What he is doing is thus tied to a goal striven for, which may or may not in fact be attained. Jones' working on the puzzle may be fruitless; it may be too hard for him. He may succeed and, moreover, do a fine job in painting his house and he may, furthermore, be successful in teaching Smith how to work the saw. In each case, the activity engaged in is oriented toward some goal defining its success and normally requiring extended effort for its attainment. In each case, too, such attainment provides one index of proficiency.

Now one may, of course, try to do many things, not all which are themselves activities which involve further tryings. One may, for example, try to sit (on a particular chair), or try to breathe (in a room with little oxygen or with an injured lung) or try to stroll (but be interrupted by unexpected guests). Such tryings are themselves oriented toward goals and may or may not be successful. It does not follow that sitting, breathing and strolling are species of trying or involve trying generally. One cannot try to sit without trying but we often sit without trying.

It is, furthermore, true that on particular occasions sitting itself, for example, may be associated *in some way* with trying. A man may be sitting in an effort to relax and catch his breath, knowing that too much exercise is bad for his heart. Nevertheless, people often do sit without trying thereby to relax or to do anything at all. To describe someone as sitting is not, in itself, to convey that he is trying to accomplish something in particular. By contrast, to describe someone as working on a puzzle is to convey that he is trying to solve it, to describe someone as painting his house is normally to convey that he is trying to get it painted, to say of someone that he is teaching a pupil how to work an electric saw is ordinarily to convey that he is trying to get him to learn how to work it.

One misunderstanding must here be forestalled. To work on a puzzle all afternoon is not, in every case, to try to solve it during the afternoon. The puzzle may be a very difficult one and known to be difficult, and the man working on it may have no hope of solving it in a few hours; he may in fact not be trying to solve it in a few hours. But he cannot be said to have been working on it even during the afternoon unless what he was doing was done in an effort to solve it, with or without some special time restriction. Similarly, one may be painting one's house all day without trying to get it painted by night-fall. But if one were not trying to get it painted at all, ever, one could hardly be said, without considerable qualification, to have spent the day painting one's house. Finally, learning to operate an electric saw may in fact require many lessons. Jones may thus be teaching Smith for an hour or two without trying to get him to learn the operation of the saw in an hour or two. But, unless what Jones does is done in the attempt to get Smith to learn its operation, he cannot well be said, in normal circumstances, to be teaching him how to operate an electric saw. The goal of an activity, in sum, may lie beyond the boundaries of the activity or some segment of it or may lack temporal conditions altogether. Nevertheless, engaging in the activity involves trying, generally.

Finally, it should be noted that teaching has here been said normally to involve an effort to achieve learning, but the converse is, as a matter of fact, false. Efforts to achieve learning cannot generally be said to involve teaching. . . . Thus, though the achievement of learning is indispensable to teaching success, it is not in itself sufficient; the learning must, in addition, be accomplished in the appropriate manner.

That teaching, as normally understood, is an activity, requiring effort and allowing for the exercise and development of proficiency, and oriented toward a goal that may lie beyond any segment of it, we have already seen. We must now try to make clearer its temporal characteristics. As an activity, teaching takes time. Suppose I told you I had been teaching John, and you asked, "When?" If I said, "Yesterday, at exactly 3:15 p.m., but neither before nor after," this answer would be thought absurd. Teaching is no instantaneous occurrence, like a thunderbolt or the flash of a falling star across the sky. Thus the question, "At exactly what moment were you engaged in teaching John?" makes no obvious sense, while "For how long were you busy teaching John?" is a perfectly legitimate question.[28]

It should now be noted that the question, "For how long have you been teaching John?" may receive, roughly, two sorts of answers. One answer may refer to relatively short intervals, for example "two hours." Another answer may refer to longer intervals, for example, "Three weeks," or "Two and a half years." Let us call all such intervals 'teaching-intervals' and notice that not every part of every teaching-interval is also a teaching-interval. If Jones has been teaching Smith how to drive an automobile, for the last three weeks, he has still, surely, not been teaching him, even during these last three weeks, while Smith has been having his lunch, during his working hours, or while he has been asleep or visiting friends. Rather, this three-week interval is characterized by a certain pattern of relatively unitary teaching-intervals, which we may here call 'lessons.'

If a continuous teaching-interval is one all of whose interval parts are themselves teaching-intervals of the same sort, then we may here construe a lesson as a continuous teaching-interval that is not itself part of some other continuous teaching-interval. A patterned sequence of lessons may then go to make up a complex teaching-interval such as a course of instruction or part of such a course. Though lessons are smaller than courses, every lesson is still an interval and not a moment, despite the fact that such important happenings as a pupil's seeing the point may indeed be momentary events highlighting the lessons during which they occur.

Let us now attend to the single lesson. What characterizes teaching during the lesson? What must we observe in order to decide that what is going on before us is a case of teaching? We have already stressed that teaching is an activity involving the attempt to achieve a certain sort of learning within certain restrictions of manner. But the implications of this point deserve to be spelled out in answer to the questions posed above.

For it is often supposed that activities are all construable as distinctive patterns of bodily movement. We have already denied that

---

[28] Related questions are discussed in Z. Vendler, "Verbs and Times," *The Philosophical Review* (April 1957), 66:143.

everything expressible in verb forms, as a truth about anyone refers to some activity. Surely it takes little further reflection to see that some such descriptions are not readily amenable to analysis into statements about movement. That Jones now owns 740 acres in Texas is completely independent of his present patterns of bodily movement. That he has just turned 45 is equally independent of his present motions, though, presumably, some general connection with his physiological condition may be expected. Such cases are relatively easy to segregate, however, and to label 'states,' in order to succumb to the temptation to maintain that activities, by contrast, *are* all construable as distinctive patterns of bodily movement. For activities, so the argument runs, are after all things we do, and what is doing but effecting some change in the environment by producing some movement?

The latter argument is, indeed, plausible but nevertheless misguided. It is, to begin with, true that the states in question are *not* normally classified as things we do. The question, "What is he doing now?" can hardly be answered by "Owning 740 acres in Texas" or "Just turning 45." It is, further, true that of the things that do answer this question, *some* are readily seen to refer to distinctive patterns of bodily movement. For example, "Just sitting," "Breathing regularly" (said by a nurse of a patient), and "Strolling through the park," are all appropriate answers and indicate some pattern of movement (where this is taken broadly as including posture or orientation as well as motion).

It is, however, also true that other appropriate answers to the question "What is he doing now?" include, for example, "Working on a geometry problem," an activity-description which turns out quite resistant to the attempt to interpret it as referring to some distinctive pattern of movements, as we shall try to show in a moment. The point to see now is that 'doing' is a broad category including things that *prima facie*, at least, are construable as movement patterns as well as things that are not. It is this fact that undermines the argument that activities must be patterns of movement since they are things we do.

But this fact must be examined concretely by reference to examples. Let us compare the case of breathing with that of working on a geometry problem, both admittedly doings, in contrast to what were above called 'states.' How is it possible to tell that a person is breathing during a given interval? We observe a certain repetitive pattern of movement associated with the sequence of air intake and expulsion during the interval. Compare the case of a boy working on a geometry problem during a given interval. He must, of course, be doing something reasonable with the aim of solving the problem. To be working on it, he must be trying as well as doing. What is observably done may, furthermore, vary with the situation, and will be associated with reflection in any event. To know that the boy before us is really working on a geometry problem and not simply playing with the paper, we need to judge that he is in fact thinking but, furthermore, we need to judge that whatever he is doing involves the hope of solving a problem. To judge that he is thinking is already to go beyond his manifest bodily movements (though not perhaps beyond certain unobserved internal changes). To judge what he is trying to do, moreover, we should ordinarily have to go beyond his bodily movements during the present interval. We may, for example, know that he is enrolled in a geometry course at school, that he has been assigned the problem as homework, that the solution is to be handed in the next day, that he has always turned in his homework promptly in the past, that he has frequently expressed the desire to major in mathematics.

All these external items of information are clues to his present intent in the light of which we interpret what he is doing (including his present movements) as "Working on the problem." His observable motions might be any of an indefinite number. He may pace the floor, stare out the window, look at a diagram, turn the paper sideways, frown, etc. Each of these motions is, furthermore, frequently duplicated in cases having nothing to do with working on a geometry problem. None is thus either a necessary or a sufficient condition of such working. (It follows that all taken together cannot be necessary and that all taken alternatively cannot be sufficient.) Here, then, is a case of an activity that is not identifiable with some distinctive pattern of movements despite the fact that it is a "doing," something done. Aside from the fact that thinking is involved, the doing of the interval requires interpretation in terms of its environing context.

Returning now to the previous questions concerning teaching during the single lesson, it seems obvious that the case is parallel to that of working on a geometry problem during a given interval. Teaching, too, involves trying as well as doing—trying to get someone to learn something. Here too, what is observably done in the way of patterns of movement varies indefinitely and is duplicated in contexts where no teaching is involved at all. The teacher may talk or he may be silent, he may write or he may not, he may ask questions or not, he may use special materials or equipment or he may not. Anything of this sort, furthermore, may be done by people not engaged in teaching. Whether a man is teaching or just criticizing, meditating, arguing, sulking, entertaining, etc., is thus not something that can be read off directly from the movements of the teacher during the lesson. Aside from the question of ascertaining the teacher's thinking, the interpretation of what is done during the lesson depends on the intent with which it is done and the determination of such intent varies with information about the lesson's context. Teaching cannot thus be construed as some distinctive pattern of movements executed by the teacher.

In the light of this analysis, it appears that attempts to think of teaching in extreme behavioristic terms are, at best, ambiguous and, at worst, totally misguided. Returning to the geometry example, it may plausibly be argued that the boy has, in fact, not solved the problem unless he can produce a proof in stated or written form. Proofs can be checked for validity, once produced. In this weak sense, it may be admitted that "behavioristic" evidence (with respect to the stated or written product of the boy's motions) enters into our judgment as to the success of his activity. It does not follow that the *production* of proofs can be generally characterized in advance, that we can say generally what pattern of speaking or writing movements constitutes a sufficient condition for problem-solution in geometry or mathematics. That such a characterization is impossible is demonstrable on mathematical grounds alone. This situation is general in science as well, where, though theories, once produced, may be evaluated as to their scientific worth, we have no general rules for the production of worthwhile theories. To think of problem-solving as a complex sequence of movements governed by rule is thus a myth.

It surely does not follow that the boy's mere working on the problem (as distinct from his solving it) can be construed as such a sequence. It is mistaken to suppose that learning geometry is a matter of mastering some distinctive pattern of movements or that teaching geometry consists in prescribing the movements to be made.

Analogously, that a given instance of teaching activity has been successful in achieving learning may plausibly be argued to admit of behavioral test in the form of some standard examination of pupils' knowledge, skills, or attitudes. It does not follow that teaching may be described as a standard pattern of movements even where it is successful, let alone where it is not. It is thus mistaken to think that one may learn to teach by mastering some distinctive pattern of movements, or that we can teach people to teach by prescribing such a pattern for them, formulated in general rules. What can reasonably be done in the way of teaching people to teach presents, indeed, a crucial problem. Suffice it for the present to remark that whatever rules can profitably be applied here are likely to be comparable to rules profitably used in the teaching of geometry or science rather than to rules of spelling.

To conclude this phase of our discussion, if we are to decide whether or not Jones is engaged in teaching activity during a specified interval, we can neither rely merely on one momentary observation nor can we rely merely on observations of Jones' movements during the interval in question. Rather, in the light of information that normally goes beyond the interval in question, we have to see whether what Jones is doing is aimed at getting someone to learn something, whether it is not unreasonably thought to be likely to achieve the learning aimed at, and whether it falls within the restrictions of manner peculiar to teaching as ordinarily understood,—in particular, whether acknowledgment of the alleged pupil's judgment is made, whether, e.g. the pupil is not systematically precluded from asking 'How?' 'Why?' or 'On what grounds?'

Thomas F. Green
Syracuse University

IV. A TOPOLOGY
OF THE TEACHING CONCEPT

A. THE TEACHING CONTINUUM

A concept is a rule. When someone learns a concept, without exception, what he has learned is a rule, a rule of language, or more generally, a rule of behavior. But some of the rules we observe in action and
speaking are enormously complicated. Some are "open textured" in
the sense that they do not specify with accuracy and precision what is
permitted under the rule and what is not. These are the kinds of rules
which are vague. They circumscribe the limits of vague concepts.

We can imagine what a vague concept is like by picturing a modern
painting in which the different colors are blurred, one blending into
another in degrees more imperceptible and gradual even than those
which we discover in the spectrum. Such a painting, when viewed at a
distance, clearly possesses a certain order among its several parts.
There is a pattern of light and colors which constitutes the structure
of the figures in the painting, but which when seen in close proximity,
conceals the order of the painting.

How could we draw a clear and precise representation of what is
found in such a painting? Here is a certain place where the colors
change from red to orange and thence to yellow. Yet we cannot, with
any certitude, point to a place and say at that point the color ceases to
be red and becomes orange, or ceases to be orange and becomes yellow.
Any attempt to specify precisely where the colors change, any attempt
to eliminate the delicate blending of one color into another, would
misrepresent the order or pattern of the painting. There are many

points at which such a line can be drawn. They would all be equally right and all equally wrong.

A vague concept is like such a picture. It is a rule which is enormously complicated, and a part of its complication arises for no other reason than that it is not precise. It allows differences of opinion and differences of judgment at precisely those blurring points where people try to specify where one color begins and another leaves off. Nonetheless, the difficulty of making such differences precise does not mean that there is no order, or that we cannot find it. It means simply that we must not insist on too much precision in the order that we find.

We can, in fact, give a description of such a picture without sacrificing anything in the way of a faithful representation. For if we discover that there are two patches of paint which can be cut out and substituted one for another without in any way changing the picture, then we would be justified in saying that these two patches are related in a certain sense, namely, in the sense that they are exactly similar. And if we discovered that the color in the space intervening between them could be reproduced by imperceptibly and gradually blending the pigment in each of these patches with some second color in ever increasing proportions, then we would be justified in saying that we understand, in a different sense, *how* these two patches of color are related. We would have specified the rule which will suffice to relate the two patches of color. In this fashion we could develop a topology of such a canvas, showing by what rule each point on the canvas is related to every other point by the gradual blending of the pigments. Thus we could reveal the structure of the painting without converting it into a line drawing.

The concept of teaching is like such a blurred picture. It is a vague concept. Its boundaries are not clear. However accurately we may describe the activity of teaching there will, and always must, remain certain troublesome border-line cases. In admitting this, the point is not that we have failed to penetrate the darkness and to discover that juncture at which an activity ceases to be teaching and becomes something else. The point is rather that beneath the darkness there is simply no such precise discrimination to be found. There is therefore an initial presumption against the credibility of any analysis which yields precise criteria, which, without a trace of uncertainty assign to every case a clear identity.

We can, nonetheless, describe the structure of the teaching concept, or if you wish, map its terrain, by standing at a distance and by asking not about teaching itself, but about such patches or parts of teaching as training, indoctrinating, conditioning, showing and instructing. We need not insist that the blur between these patches be removed. We need only show how they are related and how the gradual transition from one to the other may be reproduced. When we have done that, we will have drawn a map of the teaching concept; we will have described a rule or complex set of rules which formulates the structure of the concept.

At the outset, one must recognize then, that the concept of teaching is molecular. That is, as an activity, teaching can best be understood not as a single activity, but as a whole family of activities within which some members appear to be of more central significance than others. For example, there is an intimate relation between teaching and training which can be observed in many ways. There are, for example, contexts in which the word "teaching" may be substituted for "training" without any change of meaning. One reason for this is that teaching is often conceived to involve the formation of habit, and training is a method of shaping habit. Thus, when engaged in training, we may often say with equal propriety that we are engaged in teaching. The two concepts are closely related.

Nonetheless teaching and training are not identical. Training is only a part of teaching. There are contexts in which it would be a rank distortion to substitute the one concept for the other. For example, it is more common, and perhaps more accurate, to speak of training an animal than to speak of teaching him. I do not mean there is no such thing as teaching a dog. I mean only that it is more accurate in this context to speak of training. We can, indeed, teach a dog to fetch, to heel, to point, and to pursue. There is in fact a common saying that you cannot teach an old dog new tricks. The use of the word "teaching" in each of these cases has its explanation. It has to do with the fact that the actions of a trained dog are expressive of intelligence; they involve obedience to orders. Indeed, a well trained dog is one which has passed "obedience trials."

But the intelligence displayed in such cases is limited, and it is this which renders the education of an animal more akin to training than to teaching. What should we think of a trainer of dogs attempting to explain his orders to an animal, giving reasons for them, presenting evidence of a kind that would tend to justify them? The picture is absurd. Dogs do not ask "Why?" They do not ask for reasons for a certain rule or order. They do not require explanation or justification. It is this limitation of intelligence which we express by speaking of training rather than teaching in such circumstances. Moreover, those rare occasions in which animals most clearly display intelligence are precisely those in which they appear to ask "Why?" They are the occasions when they do precisely what they have been trained *not* to do, or when they do *not* do what they have been trained to do. The horse, trained to pull the carriage, saves his master's life in the darkness of the night by stopping at the edge of the washed out bridge and refusing to go on. The dog trained not to go into the street, is killed because he rushed into the path of a truck to push a child to safety. On such occasions, it is as though the animal had obeyed an order which was not given. It is as though he had given himself a reason for acting contrary to his training.

I am not concerned whether this, or something like it, is a correct explanation of such remarkable happenings. I am concerned only to observe that training resembles teaching insofar as it is aimed at actions which display intelligence. In this respect, training has a position of central importance in that congerie of activities we include in teaching. Ordinarily, however, the kind of intelligence aimed at in training is limited. What it excludes is the process of asking questions, weighing evidence and, in short, demanding and receiving a justification of rules, principles, or claims of fact. In proportion as training is aimed at a greater and greater display of intelligence, it more and more clearly resembles teaching, and one of the clues as to how closely training approaches teaching is the degree to which it involves explanations, reasons, argument, and weighing evidence. It is because training sometimes approaches this point, that we can in many cases substitute the word "teaching" for the word "training" without any change in meaning.

This point is strengthened when we consider what happens in proportion as training is aimed less and less at the display of intelligence. In that case, the concept fades off imperceptibly into what we would commonly call conditioning. It is natural to speak of teaching a dog to fetch, to heel, to walk in time to music. It is more of a distortion to speak of teaching a dog to salivate at the sound of a bell. It is in precisely this latter context that we speak of conditioning. Conditioning does not aim at an intelligent performance of some act.[1] Insofar as

---

[1] There may be circumstances, however, in which it would be intelligent, i.e., wise, to "teach" with the aim of producing a conditioned response.

training does not aim at the display of intelligence, it resembles conditioning more and teaching less. Thus, we can see that training is an activity which is conceptually of more central importance to the concept of teaching than is conditioning. We teach a dog to fetch; we condition him to salivate. And the difference is a difference in the degree of intelligence displayed.

Instruction also must be included in the family of activities related to teaching. Instructing, in fact, is so closely bound to teaching that the phrase "giving instruction" seems only another way of saying "teaching." There seems to be no case of an activity we could describe as "giving instruction" which we could not equally and more simply describe as teaching. Nonetheless, teaching and giving instruction are not the same thing. For there are almost endless instances of teaching which do not involve instruction. For example, it is acceptable, and even correct, to speak of *teaching* a dog to heel, to sit, or to fetch. It is, however, less acceptable, more imprecise, and perhaps even incorrect to speak of *instructing* a dog in sitting and fetching.

But why, in such contexts, is it more awkward to speak of instructing than to speak of teaching? We need not go far to discover the answer. When we train a dog, we give an order and then push and pull and give reward or punishment. We give the order to sit and then push on the hindquarters precisely because we cannot explain the order. We cannot elaborate its meaning. It is precisely this limitation of intelligence or communication which disposes us to speak of training a dog rather than instructing him. What we seek to express by the phrase "giving instruction" is precisely what we seek to omit by the word "training." Instruction seems, at heart, to involve a kind of conversation, the object of which is to give reasons, weigh evidence, justify, explain, conclude, and so forth. It is true that whenever we are involved in giving instruction, it follows that we are engaged in teaching; but it is not true that whenever we are engaged in teaching, we are giving instruction.

This important difference between training and instructing may be viewed in another way. To the extent that instructing necessarily involves a kind of conversation, a giving of reasons, evidence, objections and so on, it is an activity of teaching allied more closely to the acquisition of knowledge and belief than to the promotion of habits and modes of behavior. Training, on the contrary, has to do more with forming modes of habit and behavior and less with acquiring knowledge and belief. Instructing, in short, is more closely related to the quest for understanding. We can train people to do certain things without making any effort to bring them to an understanding of what they do. It is, however, logically impossible to instruct someone without at the same time attempting to bring him to some understanding. What this means, stated in its simplest and most ancient terms, is that instructing always involves matters of truth and falsity whereas training does not. This is another reason for observing that instructing has more to do with matters of belief and knowledge, and training more with acquiring habits or modes of behaving. It is not therefore a bit of archaic nonsense that teaching is essentially the pursuit of truth. It is, on the contrary, an enormously important insight. The pursuit of truth is central to the activity of teaching because giving instruction is central to it. That, indeed, is the purpose of the kind of conversation indigenous to the concept of giving instruction. If giving instruction involves giving reasons, evidence, argument, justification, then instruction is essentially related to the search for truth.

The point is not, therefore, that instructing necessarily requires communication. The point is rather that it requires a certain *kind* of communication, and that kind is the kind which includes giving reasons, evidence, argument, etc., in order to approach the truth. The importance of this fact can be seen if we consider what happens when the conversation of instruction is centered less and less upon this kind of communication. It takes no great powers of insight to see that in proportion as the conversation of instruction is less and less characterized by argument, reasons, objections, explanations, and so forth, in proportion as it is less and less directed toward an apprehension of truth, it more and more closely resembles what we call indoctrination. Indoctrination is frequently viewed as a method of instruction. Indeed, we sometimes use the word "instruction" to include what we quite openly confess is, in fact, indoctrination. Nonetheless, indoctrination is a substantially different thing from instruction, and what is central to this difference is precisely that it involves a different kind of conversation and therefore is differently related to matters of truth.

We can summarize the essential characteristics of these differences by saying that indoctrination is to conditioning as beliefs are to habits. That is to say, we may indoctrinate people to *believe* certain things, but we condition them always to *do* certain things. We do not indoctrinate persons to certain modes of behavior any more than we condition them to certain kinds of beliefs. But the important thing is to observe that *insofar as* conditioning does not aim at an expression of intelligent doing, neither does indoctrination aim at an expression of intelligent believing. Conditioning is an activity which can be used to establish certain modes of behavior quite apart from their desirability. It aims simply to establish them. If a response to a certain stimulus is trained or conditioned, or has become a fixed habit, it will be displayed in the fact that the same stimulus will produce the same response even when the person admits it would be better if he responded otherwise. This is an unintelligent way of behaving. In an analogous way, indoctrination is aimed at an unintelligent way of holding beliefs. Indoctrination aims simply at establishing certain beliefs so that they will be held quite apart from their truth, their explanation, or their foundation in evidence. As a practical matter, indoctrinating involves certain conversation, but it does not involve the kind of conversation central to the activity of giving instruction. Thus, as the teaching conversation becomes less related to the pursuit of truth, it becomes less an activity of instruction and more a matter of indoctrination. We may represent these remarks schematically:

THE TEACHING CONTINUUM

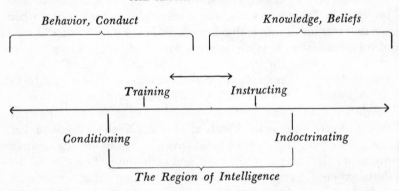

The diagram is not meant to suggest that the distinctions between conditioning, training, instructing and indoctrinating are perfectly clear and precise. On the contrary, each of these concepts, like the teaching concept itself, is vague. Each blends imperceptibly into its neighbor. It is as with the well-known case of baldness. We cannot say with precision and accuracy at precisely what point a man becomes bald. There is nonetheless a distinction, clear enough in its extremities, between a bald head and a hairy head. One might say that the difference is a matter of degree. But if the difference between conditioning and training or between instructing and indoctrinating is simply a difference of degree, then one must ask, "What is it that differs in degree?" The fact is that instructing and indoctrinating are different in kind, but the respects in which they differ may be exemplified in different degrees. Thus, we may be uncertain in many concrete cases whether the conversation of a teaching sequence more nearly resembles instructing or indoctrinating. But it does not follow from this that the difference between them is obscure, that we are uncertain about it or that they differ only in degree. It follows only that in such specific instances the criteria that mark the difference, though perfectly clear in themselves, are neither clearly exemplified nor clearly absent.

A parallel example may suffice to make this clearer. To lie is to tell a falsehood with the intent to deceive. But now consider the following circumstances. Two brothers go to bed on the eve of one's birthday. He whose birthday is coming wishes to know what in the way of gifts the next day may hold in store for him. So he questions, prods, cajoles, and teases his brother to tell him. But he receives only the unsatisfactory but truthful answer from his brother that he does not know. And so the teasing continues and sleep is made impossible. The only recourse for the weary one is to invent a lie. It must, however, be a lie that is believable. It must satisfy and yet must be most assuredly a lie. And so he says what is most improbable, "You will get a bicycle." But now suppose they discover on the morning after that indeed the principal gift is a bicycle. The question might arise, did the brother lie or did he not? If the answer is "Yes," the difficulty arises that what he said was in fact the truth. If the answer is "No," the fact will arise that he intended to deceive. A case may be built for both answers, because in this illustration, the criteria for lying and for truth telling are mixed. The case is neither one nor the other. It does not follow, however, that the difference between lying and truth telling is obscure. Such examples show only that the criteria which mark the difference may be in more or less degree fulfilled. It shows there is a degree of vagueness present, a point at which we cannot decide.

And so it is in the present case. The concept of teaching, as we normally use it, includes within its limits a whole family of activities, and we can recognize that some of these are more centrally related to teaching than others. We have no difficulty, for example, in agreeing that instructing and certain kinds of training are activities which belong to teaching. We may have more difficulty, and some persons more than others, in deciding whether conditioning and indoctrinating legitimately belong to teaching. There is, in short, a region on this continuum at which we may legitimately disagree, because there will be many contexts in which the criteria which tend to distinguish teaching and conditioning or teaching and indoctrination will not be clearly exemplified. Thus, there is an area of uncertainty on this continuum, an area of vagueness neither to be overcome nor ignored, but respected and preserved.

Nonetheless, were we to extend this continuum, we would discover another region of agreement. For we would surely stretch a point too far were we to extend the line on the left and include such activities as intimidation and physical threat, or on the right and include such things as exhorting, propagandizing and just plain lying. The continuum would look like this:

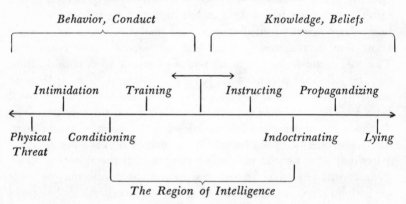

THE TEACHING CONTINUUM EXPANDED

We would have to strain and struggle to include within the teaching family such things as extortion, lying and deceit. The point is not that such things *cannot* be included among the assemblage of teaching activities. The point is rather that to do so would require an extension and distortion of the concept of teaching. It is clear in any case that such activities are less central to the concept of teaching than conditioning and indoctrination, and that these are, in turn, less central than training and instruction. Thus as we extend the extremities of this continuum we depart from a region of relative uncertainty and enter a segment within which we can agree with relative ease. Lying,

propagandizing, slander and threat of physical violence are not teaching activities, although they may be ways of influencing persons'
beliefs or shaping their behavior. We know in fact, that these activities are excluded from the concept of teaching with as much certainty
as we know that training and instructing are included. This shows
approximately where the region of vagueness occurs in the concept of
teaching. It occurs in respect to matters of behavior, somewhere between the activities of training and conditioning, and in respect to
matters of knowledge and belief, it occurs somewhere between instructing and indoctrinating. The most central properties of the concept of teaching are revealed, in short, within the limits of what we
have called the region of intelligence. Or, to put the matter in another
way, we can say that teaching has to do primarily with the relation
between thought and action.

It is a matter of no consequence that there have been societies which
have extended the concept of teaching beyond this limit of vagueness
and have thus included even the most remote extremities of this continuum. That propaganda, lies, threats, and intimidation have been
used as methods of education is not doubted. But the conclusion warranted by this fact is not that teaching includes such activities, but that
education may. Propaganda, lies, and threats are more or less effective
means of influencing and shaping beliefs and patterns of behavior.
It follows that teaching is not the only method of education. It does
not follow that the use of propaganda, lies and threats are methods
of teaching.

The concept of teaching is thus a molecular concept. It includes a
congerie of activities. In order to more clearly understand the concept
it may suffice to simply describe in schematic form what are the logical
properties most central to this family of activities and to display in
what respects other less central activities do or do not bear the marks
of teaching. In this way we may gain in clarity without doing violence
to the vagueness inherent in the concept. At the same time, we may
avoid importing some obscure and *a priori* normative definition of
teaching.

B. THE TEACHING CONTINUUM
AND THE TOPOLOGY OF BELIEF SYSTEMS

Such a topology of the teaching concept is partially displayed in
the teaching continuum. In order the better to see what is implicit
in this continuum, it is necessary, or at any rate useful, to introduce

another topological model, or set of models, having to do primarily with the right-hand side of the continuum. That is to say, this topology has to do not with the structure of the teaching concept, but with the structure of belief systems. It is related to the concept of teaching, however, because teaching has less to do with *what* we believe and more to do with *how* we believe; and this contrast is best displayed in the structure of belief systems.[2]

This contrast between what beliefs we hold and how we hold them is not, however, altogether obvious. For it may seem, initially at least, that a person must either believe a thing or not, and that there can be no question as to *how* he believes it. A belief, after all, is either true or doubtful, precise or muddled, clear or confused. But these differences all have to do with the belief itself and not with the *way* it is believed. One might suppose there cannot be different ways of believing a thing as there are different ways of planting corn or skinning a cat. When a person believes something, he believes it to be true, and in addition to arriving at some decision on its truth, he does not need to decide also *how* to go about believing it.

There are, nonetheless, certain adjectives which appear in belief statements but which do not qualify the truth or falsity, clarity or precision of the belief. They have to do instead with the *way* we believe something. They delineate, as it were, a "style" of belief. We can, for example, believe something strongly or not, with passion or not, for good reasons or not. Two persons may hold the same belief with a different measure of strength, with more or less adequate reasons, or on more or less adequate evidence. They may, on the contrary, believe different things with equal strength, reasons, or evidence.

These adjectives of belief style fall roughly into two categories. In the first, there are those which have to do with the way beliefs are held in relation to each other. In the second class are those words which describe the way beliefs are held in relation to evidence or reasons. To understand these differences, we have to recognize that people seldom if ever hold to a belief in isolation, in total independence of other beliefs. Each of us, in fact, possesses a whole system of beliefs, and we can understand that in this system there may occur different arrangements. Thus, two persons may hold to similar beliefs and yet they may hold them in quite different arrangements. Thus the order

---

[2] The following account of belief systems is suggested by, but not derivable from nor identifiable with, the views of Milton Rokeach. In many ways this account goes beyond what Rokeach has done, and goes beyond it in a way he would find unacceptable. See his *The Open and Closed Mind* (New York: Basic Books Incorporated, 1960).

of one's beliefs is a property of belief systems conceptually distinct from their content, and this can be described as a contrast between the beliefs we hold and how we hold them.

For example, in the order of anyone's beliefs there are quite often identifiable relations of a logical sort. That is to say, there are always certain beliefs which people may tend to reject because they understand them to be logically incompatible with others they accept. The point is not that such beliefs *are* logically inconsistent, but only that they are thought so. Similarly, we can identify some beliefs which a person may tend to accept because he finds them implied by others he accepts or consistent with others he accepts. Given any three beliefs in a system we shall say that if C is held to as implied by B, then B is primitive in respect to C. But if B in turn is held to as implied by A, then B, which is primitive in respect to C, is derivative in respect to A. When a belief has the status of a primitive belief and is not itself held to be derivative from any other belief, then we may say it is a primary primitive belief.

In short, the concept of primitive and derivative beliefs is a quasi-logical concept. That is to say, it has nothing to do with the actual objective logical relation between beliefs. But it does have to do with the logical order they receive in a belief system. A primitive belief is one which is not itself questioned. In this respect it resembles a postulate. It is itself appealed to in determining the acceptability of other beliefs. A belief which is seen to be implied by a primitive belief will *tend* to be more acceptable. One which is seen to contradict a primitive belief will *tend* to be rejected. A primitive belief then has the status of an arbiter, so to speak, in determining which beliefs can be received and which must be rejected. But the important point is that this adjudicative function is performed on the basis of a logical claim. It is the claim that what is implied by a truth must be true; what is contradicted by a truth must be false.[3]

---

[3] See Leon Festinger, *A Theory of Cognitive Dissonance* (Evanston, Illinois: Row, Peterson and Company, 1957). His thesis roughly is that when one receives a message which is dissonant with an established belief held by a person, then one or more of three different things may happen, either the message will be rejected and some reasons developed to justify its rejection, or it will be modified so as to become "consonant" with the belief system and therefore suitable for internalization, or finally, the belief system itself may be modified so as to become "consonant" with the message. Festinger is not always clear concerning the meaning of the terms "consonant" and "dissonant", but they are reminiscent of the logical notions of "consistent" and "inconsistent" (p. 2), and are actually given "a more formal conceptual definition" (p. 3) in terms of negation and the phrase "follows from". Although his discussion lacks precision at the level of definition, there is no doubt that he is pointing to the fact that belief systems do have a logical structure of the kind I have tried to sketch.

But this relationship between primary and derivative beliefs is not a fixed or stable one, nor is it the objective order which logicians may establish between propositions. It has to do with the logical order which beliefs receive in a system. It has long been observed that men have the untidy disposition to hold in logical relation beliefs which are in fact wholly independent. The objective order of beliefs discoverable through logic, is based upon their content and structure. It has to do with *what* is believed. But the order we are concerned to describe has to do with the order beliefs may be given. It can be described only as having to do with *how* they are believed.

The second point to observe is really a facet of what has been said already. It is simply that belief systems are in many respects not logical systems at all. When, for example, the theory of evolution is found by some person to conflict with some logically primitive belief concerning the authority of scripture, it is true that one or the other belief will *tend* to be rejected or modified; but we must ask *which* it shall be, the belief in evolution or the belief in the authority of scripture. And this question has to do less with the logical structure of a belief system than with its psychological or spacial order. It is not uncommon for students in the course of study to discover that they must alter certain of their beliefs and cancel out others altogether. The facts of social life and the order of institutions may conflict with one's idealized conceptions of the world. Some cherished myths regarding our national heroes may become shattered in the pursuit of the truth about our history. If one is to live in the company of others, some cherished standards of judging them may have to be abandoned along with some treasured estimates of one's self. It is often with respect to some beliefs an easy thing to change and with respect to others wholly beyond the realm of possibility. A belief which one person may be quite prepared to doubt, another may be incapable of questioning.

Thus some beliefs are more important than others, and the measure of their importance, in this sense, is not whether they are logically primitive but whether they are psychologically central. Thus, we can visualize a belief system as having a spacial dimension, as having the structure of a set of concentric circles. Within the core circle will be those beliefs held with greatest psychological strength, those which we are most prone to accept without question, and, therefore, least able to debate openly and least able to change. As we move from circle to circle toward the perimeter there will be distributed those beliefs which we hold with progressively less strength and are more prepared to examine, discuss, and alter.

Psychologically central beliefs do not cluster together because they are logically primitive. It is quite conceivable, in fact, that beliefs could be logically derivative and yet psychologically central. Beliefs which are quite independent in the logical dimension of a belief system may nonetheless be related by the fact that they are "core" beliefs. Whether a belief is central or peripheral has, therefore, little to do with its content; it has to do not so much with what a person believes, as with how he believes it. Thus, the same belief may be psychologically central to one person and peripheral to another. The spacial location of a belief is determined not by its logical properties, but by the manner of its psychological possession.

A belief system is not a logical system. It is not at all uncommon that men hold strongly to certain beliefs which if ever set side by side would clearly conflict. But until they be set side by side, and their inconsistency revealed, there need be no problem in believing both. Indeed, two beliefs equally central psychologically, may be logically incompatible. Thus one may hold certain central convictions concerning matters of economics—that competition among men is the only basis for social progress, that individual initiative is the supreme requirement for merit, that a man is entitled to keep what he can secure, that if a person does not "succeed," he has no one to blame but himself. Similarly, one may hold to a set of beliefs in matters of public morality—that only by cooperation among men can society be improved, that one must be charitable in assisting those who are less fortunate, that a good member of society is one who does not "take advantage" of his neighbors.

Such conflicting sets of beliefs may all be held as psychologically central. This is possible because we tend to order our beliefs in little clusters encrusted about, as it were, by a protective shield which prevents any cross-fertilization among them or any confrontation between them. Thus we may praise the value of competition as an article of economic faith and the necessity for cooperation as a fundamental demand of social ethics. In this way we can hold psychologically central, certain beliefs which are at many points logically incompatible. This is perfectly possible provided we never permit our cluster of economic beliefs to influence our ethical convictions or permit our ethical beliefs to influence our economic thought. We can do this effectively by protecting certain clusters of beliefs by a hard coating as the germ of a seed is protected from the corrosive influences of the winter. This impregnable shield appears disguised as a belief itself. "Ethics has nothing to do with business" or "Religion ought to stay out of politics." A student for example, may possess a religious faith which militates against the demands of inquiry. He may nonetheless, be a successful student provided he never permits his religious faith to influence his life as a student, and conversely never permits his life as a student to influence his understanding of his religion. Such a segregation of concerns can be accomplished by adopting certain beliefs. "Matters of faith are beyond the reach of reason to appraise." Or, again, it is not uncommon to find those who devote their lives to scientific study and yet hold to a religion which is fundamentally a matter of magic. "Science is one thing and religion is quite another."

We may therefore identify a third dimension of belief systems. First, there is a logical relation between beliefs. They are primary or derivative. Secondly, there is a relation between them which has to do with their spacial location or psychological strength. But there is a third dimension in every belief system by which certain clusters of beliefs are held more or less in isolation from other clusters and protected from any relationship with other sets of beliefs. Each of these dimensions has to do not with the content of our beliefs, but with the *way* we hold them. None of these dimensions need be stable. Indeed, the belief systems of different persons can be described in relation to the ease with which different clusters of beliefs can be related, the number and nature of the logically primitive and psychologically central beliefs, the ease with which they may move from center to periphera and back, and the correspondence or lack of it between the objective logical order of beliefs and the order in which they are actually held.

There is a second way of marking this distinction between beliefs we hold and how we hold them. It has to do not with the relation between beliefs, but with their relation to evidence or reasons. When beliefs are held without regard to evidence or contrary to evidence, or apart from good reasons or the canons for testing reasons and evidence, then we may say they are held non-evidentially. It follows that beliefs held non-evidentially cannot be modified by introducing evidence or reasons or by rational criticism. When beliefs, however, are held "on the basis of" evidence or reasons, can be rationally criticised, and therefore can be modified in the light of further evidence or better reasons, then we shall say they are held evidentially.

This contrast between holding beliefs evidentially and non-evidentially corresponds closely to a fundamental point on the teaching continuum. It has to do with a conventional contrast between teaching and indoctrinating. This difference has nothing to do with the contents of beliefs. It is perfectly possible that two persons may hold to the same belief and yet one may do so evidentially and the other non-evidentially. It is possible, in other words, to indoctrinate people into the truth. The only problem is that they will not *know* that it is the truth. They will only know that it is a *correct* belief. That is to say, they will hold to certain true beliefs, but will be unable to give any adequate reasons for them, any clear account for them, or offer any sound evidence in their support beyond the logically irrelevant observation that they are commonly held beliefs. And yet we cannot be said to *know* that a belief is true, if we cannot give any reasons for it, any explanation of it or any evidence in support of it. In short, even though the beliefs one holds are true, one cannot be said to know they are true, if they are believed in this non-evidential fashion. They can only be known to be *correct* beliefs, and that is one of the features of beliefs held as a consequence of indoctrination.

But this contrast between teaching and indoctrination cuts more deeply. Consider the following context.[4] At some conferences there is a period set aside to lay out the work of the conference, to set the limits to be observed and the methods to be followed. It involves the presentation of decisions already arrived at and now presented as "the ground rules," so to speak, within which the work of the conference shall proceed. A sales conference, for example, may be concerned with the study and discussion of a single method of selling, excluding all others from consideration.

Such a period is sometimes called an orientation period. But it may also appropriately, more accurately, but less wisely, be called a period of indoctrination because of the place and function served by debate. In such a period, persons may raise questions; there may be discussion and a certain amount of disagreement expressed with decisions arrived at. This process overtly resembles the process of debate carried on for the purpose of informing and arriving at decisions. But in this context questions are raised, information given and discussion permitted only for purposes of persuasion, never for purposes of *arriving* at conclusions.

---

[4] The following illustration was suggested by a student of mine, Mr. William Lauderdale.

Both teaching and indoctrination may involve debate, questions, discussions and argument. Both appear to involve instruction, and, in that respect, there is a striking resemblance between them. But there also is a great difference. In indoctrinating, the conversation of instruction is employed only in order that fairly specific and predetermined beliefs may be set. Conflicting evidence and troublesome objections must be withheld because there is no purpose of inquiry. The conversation of instruction is adopted without its intent, without the "due regard for truth" so essential to instruction. Not every point on the teaching continuum is, therefore, equally a point where truth is significant. Indoctrination begins precisely where a concern for truth ends. In short, the intent of indoctrination is to lead people to hold beliefs as though they were arrived at by inquiry, and yet to hold them independently of any subsequent inquiry and therefore secure against the threat of change by the later introduction of conflicting reasons or conflicting evidence. The intent, in other words, is to produce persons who hold their beliefs non-evidentially.

That this is the intent of indoctrination is proved by the fact that the process of indoctrinating, unlike the process of teaching, is *logically* dispensable to success. Consider, for example, the following illustration.[5] Suppose we identify two persons, Adams and Barnes, neither of whom knows the identity of the discoverer of the American continent. Let us suppose that with Adams we present certain evidence, give explanations, enter into arguments, examine the statements of authorities, and finally Adams concludes that there are reasonably good grounds for the claim that the discoverer of the American continent was Columbus.

Let us use a different method in the case of Barnes. He is told to respond with the name "Columbus" whenever asked for the identity of the discoverer of the American continent. He is then asked the question at intervals, rewarded for the correct answer and punished in some way for a wrong answer. In this manner, he may learn to respond correctly and without hesitation.

But could we say that Barnes had been taught that Columbus discovered America? Certainly not. One reason is that at no point in such a process need it be asserted that Columbus *did* discover America. We could say that Barnes had been trained to make a certain response, a response which, by the way, need not manifest intelligence, but we

---

[5] Another student of mine, Mr. Gerald Reagan, suggested this illustration, although to make a slightly different point.

could not say he had been taught that Columbus discovered America. Indeed, he could have learned to make this response without having learned that Columbus discovered America. For this reason, we could not say that Adams and Barnes had learned the same thing, even though by certain observable measures they will appear to give the same response. What Barnes knows is how to respond. What Adams knows is that Columbus discovered America. What one knows is a skill; what the other knows is a truth—or at least a reasonably well-founded belief. But what is most important is that Adams has arrived at this knowledge or belief by a process which we call teaching, and he could not arrive at this truth or come to hold this belief as he does hold it, except by that process or by a process resembling it in certain important logical respects.

The creation of an evidential style of belief is inextricably and logically tied to the process of instruction, or to another process which closely resembles instruction. A non-evidential style of belief, however, is conceptually independent of the process by which beliefs are acquired. A belief is held non-evidentially when it is held quite apart from any reasons, evidence or canons for testing reasons and evidence; and, therefore, the process by which the belief comes to be held is logically a matter of no consequence. But when a belief is held evidentially, it is held always in relation to its grounds in reasons or evidence; and thus the process by which the belief comes to be held is logically decisive.

This is an extraordinarily important and far-reaching mark of difference between instructing and indoctrinating. It follows that insofar as teaching has to do with the acquisition of knowledge and beliefs held evidentially, it is an activity which necessarily involves instruction.

This does not imply that the way of knowing and believing aimed at in instructing can be achieved only by instruction. It does imply, however, that it can be achieved only by a process which resembles instruction in certain important respects. Study, for example, is an activity which aims at accomplishing the results of instruction; yet it does not require the presence of an instructor. Study, in short, is a method of learning and not a method of teaching. Although study is an activity more intimately related to learning than to teaching, it is nonetheless an activity which in its anatomy starkly resembles instruction. Study, as distinguished from other methods of learning—practice, drill, memorization—always involves asking questions, weighing evidence, giving and testing reasons, and so forth. The conversation of study, in short, is the same as the conversation of instruction. What is aimed at in teaching, insofar as it involves instruction, can also be accomplished by study. This fact we acknowledge when we speak of the need for independent study rather than the need for independent learning. In this way we acknowledge that study is another way of accomplishing precisely what is aimed at in teaching.

Suppose, however—to return to our example—that after extensive periods of instruction, Adams refused to acknowledge that Columbus was the discoverer of the American continent. Would it follow that we had failed in teaching? Not necessarily.[6] We would need to know *for what reasons* he refuses to assent to such a commonly held opinion. It may be, in fact, that the reasons for his judgment are better than can be offered for the more widely received opinion. He might say something like this: "There seems to be good evidence for the view that Columbus was not the first European to set foot on the American continent. Indeed, it seems a well established fact that many years before Columbus' voyage, there were visitors to this continent of some Scandinavian descent. But the visits of these people seem not to have had the far-reaching historical consequences of Columbus' discovery. If you consider the historical consequences of great importance, then one might say Columbus discovered America. But if you mean by that that this was the *first* discovery of America, then you would be mistaken."

This kind of reply would not signal the failure of instruction. It would be evidence of singular success. Instruction is an activity which has to do not with what people believe but with how they believe it. It has to do not so much with arriving at "the right answer" as with arriving at an answer on the right kind of grounds. It is no objection to point out the many areas of knowledge in which it is important to lead students to the right answer. For all that is usually pointed out is that there are many areas of knowledge in which the grounds of decision are decisive, and in which therefore there *is* a correct answer which it is important to know. Even in mathematics, however, where a "right answer" is often discoverable, a concern simply to lead students to that answer, or to equip them to find it, is a fundamentally defective kind of instruction. Even in such a formal science where

---

[6] Note, however, that a failure to get the "right answer" in the case of Barnes would constitute a failure to succeed in teaching. Indoctrination aims at inculcating the "right answer", but not necessarily for "the right reasons" or even for good reasons.

certitude is common, we are concerned that students be brought to an evidential style of knowing. To focus simply upon securing a right solution without understanding the nature of mathematical operations is the mathematical equivalent of indoctrination. Indeed, when indoctrination is seen to involve a certain style of knowing or believing, we can discover the possibility of indoctrination in nearly every area of human knowledge and not simply in those having to do with what we would more commonly call "matters of doctrine." In other words, when, in teaching, we are concerned simply to lead another person to a correct answer, but are not correspondingly concerned that they arrive at that answer on the basis of good reasons, then we are indoctrinating; we are engaged in creating a non-evidential style of belief.

There is one further curious fact to observe about the concept of indoctrination and its relation to a non-evidential way of holding beliefs. It has to do with the difficulty in identifying concrete cases of indoctrination as opposed to teaching. We have already suggested that there is an area of vagueness between instructing and indoctrinating. The difference between them is clear, but the criteria that mark the difference may, in specific instances, be mixed. For example, a person who has received his beliefs by indoctrination will be able to give reasons for them, offer evidence, and in other ways display every mark of holding his beliefs in an evidential way. But this is an illusion, albeit an illusion to which each of us, in some measure, submits. A person who is indoctrinated can sometimes give reasons and evidence for his beliefs, because as a practical matter, reasons and evidence were necessary in the process of establishing his beliefs. The difference, however, is betrayed in his *use* of reasons and evidence. He will use argument, criticism, evidence, and so forth, not as an instrument of inquiry, but as an instrument establishing what he already believes. He will display a marked incapacity to seriously consider conflicting evidence or entertain contrary reasons. That is to say, such a person will hold his beliefs as matters of ideology. It is indeed the characteristic of an ideology that it requires reason and argument, not for inquiry, but for defense. It requires reason as a weapon. This is not required for the defense of a belief held evidentially.

The point is that the differences between instruction and indoctrination, clear enough conceptually, are extraordinarily difficult to detect in specific cases. It requires, in ourselves, the capacity to discriminate between beliefs which are held evidentially and those which are not. To do this, we must not only have the capacity to detect sophistry in ourselves, but the courage to reject it when discovered, and the psychic freedom to follow where the pursuit of truth may lead. The detection of non-evidential beliefs in ourselves, therefore, requires not simply the logical skill to examine and appraise the adequacy of reasons, but the psychic freedom to give up or alter those beliefs which are non-evidential. In short, the distinction between instruction and indoctrination, easy enough to grasp intellectually, is immensely difficult to detect in practice, because it involves nothing less than the most radical examination of our belief systems in their psychological dimensions. To possess such a capacity is a mark of rare courage and honesty.

This psychic difficulty corresponds to a certain interesting logical difficulty. It is a curious but quite understandable fact that it is both grammatically and logically impossible for a person to say of himself truthfully and in the present tense, that he holds his beliefs as a consequence of indoctrination. It is something which cannot be said. Suppose I walk into a room where I find someone lying down in an attitude of blissful sleep. I ask, "Are you asleep?" Without hesitation, with clarity and firmness of voice, he answers, "I am." His answer is strong evidence that in fact he is not asleep. Similarly, if a person says with sincerity and conviction "My beliefs *are* indoctrinated." (there is no satisfactory way of putting it) it must follow that his beliefs are no longer held as a consequence of indoctrination only, and he is already on his way toward an evidential style of belief. Indoctrination is successful only if people *think* they hold their beliefs evidentially and in fact do not, only when they use reason as a weapon under the illusion that they are seriously inquiring. Indoctrination then is the intentional propagation of an illusion. All of us live with this illusion to some extent. Insofar as teaching is directed at matters of knowledge and belief, it involves instruction and may be described as the effort to free us from this illusion to whatever extent that is possible. Teaching might be described then as the unending effort to reconstitute the psychic structure of our ways of believing. But in order to begin, instruction presupposes that there is already a certain kind of structure of beliefs. The death of innocence is needed before teaching can begin. At this point teaching and indoctrination both become intimately related to the formation of attitudes.

To say this, however, is merely to repeat an observation at least as old as Socrates' attempt at the moral reform of Athens, namely that the beginning of inquiry is the confession of ignorance and the ensuing willingness to follow where the truth may lead. This is an attitude, a disposition, which like most other attitudes can be described as the manifestation of a certain kind of belief system, a certain way of holding beliefs. He cannot be taught who is convinced there is no truth to be appropriated or none he does not possess already. But it takes no great fund of experience to observe how rare is the capacity to admit one's ignorance, to seriously entertain new ideas, alternative ways of doing things, and to change one's point of viewing the world. Every mind is fettered to some extent, ridden with presuppositions and stereotypes which stand in the way of mental freedom. Every man knows some point at which he cannot earnestly confess his ignorance. It would come as a personal affront; it would endanger the self.

These are the points which teaching cannot touch. For teaching, insofar as it involves matters of knowledge and belief, begins with posing questions to be answered or answers to be questioned. It begins by placing such matters in the open where they cannot be avoided. But there are those who cannot allow certain questions to be raised, who cannot permit certain doubts because they touch upon themselves too directly, threaten them too deeply. In proportion as such questions are greater and greater in number, in proportion as one's psychologically central beliefs are multiplied and segregated, teaching has less and less scope for success. Teaching is ineffectual in those whose minds are enchained by prejudice or who cannot face the questions which must be raised. Teaching aims to remove these fetters; it seeks by instruction to reconstitute the order of our beliefs so that even our psychologically central beliefs are evidentially held. But in this it presupposes already some measure of psychic freedom. For instruction to proceed, it must, in effect, find some foothold from which to push back the darkness and let in the light.

It is in this sense that the practice of teaching presupposes certain attitudes, the cultivation of which is at the same time the consequence of teaching. The attitudes it presupposes, constitute that posture toward the self and toward the world which permits new questions to present themselves and new answers to be entertained. When a teacher can, in effect, find no foothold from which to proceed, he must try directly to change attitudes in order to begin teaching. The formation of attitudes is, in this sense, a precondition for teaching. It is also a consequence, however, insofar as teaching is concerned with the *way* we hold our beliefs. To the extent that it has this consequence, we may say that teaching is that activity which preeminently aims at enhancing the human capacity for action. It is concerned with the nurture of that state of being which we might describe as the posture of the pilgrim, the capacity, within limits, to tolerate an increasing measure of alienation, to be free to wander in the world.[7]

One of the clearest illustrations of the failure to teach, in this sense, is found in the Church. For in the Church, as in the political arena of our society, there are those who think the aim of teaching is to get people to hold certain specific beliefs even though the evidence does not always support them, though they are not believable to the person taught and cannot be defended on the basis of good reasons. The result of so-called Christian education is, sometimes from the perspective of the university, disastrous. Sometimes it destroys the possibility of teaching because it results in a non-evidential style of belief. There is learning in such education, but the kind of learning which results in holding beliefs so that henceforth further learning is made more difficult and further teaching rendered all but impossible.

No one who has long been a university teacher will fail to detect how often those students most at home in the Church, most articulate in matters doctrinal, are those whose minds are most bound and restricted and who are least able to learn or seriously inquire. They are often the ones least capable of doubt and most lacking in the courage to follow where the truth may lead them. They are, in short, often lacking in the moral courage which their lives as students require. Their education in the Church often has had the consequence of multiplying their "core" beliefs by an endless list of prohibitions,

---

[7] The topology of teaching helps us to discriminate between those considerations which enter as a part of the teaching activity and those which enter only as presuppositions of the teaching act. For example, there are some views of teaching which focus upon the personal relation of teacher and student, emphasize the need for mutual trust and acceptance, and thus, stress in the teaching relation those matters having to do primarily with mental health and self-understanding. Such views tend to picture the teaching activity as primarily therapeutic. Such views have nothing to do with the teaching activity, though they have much to do with satisfying the conditions without which teaching cannot succeed or even begin. In short, they deal with the presuppositions of teaching and not with its substance.

This does not mean that such views are irrelevant to what teachers are concerned to do. For there are many actual settings in which teachers, for psychological and institutional reasons, are called upon to forsake the task of teaching and attend to those matters which must be satisfied in order that teaching may begin. It ought always to be kept in mind that the "office" of teacher often requires more than a talent for teaching. It requires also that one be now a counselor, now a clinician, now a friendly guide, and another time a public relations officer. To say that these activities have to do with the presuppositions of teaching does not mean they must temporally precede the activity of teaching. It means simply that though they are always involved in the "office" of teacher, they are not logically central to the activity of teaching.

and segregating their beliefs into such well protected and isolated clusters that neither facts nor reasons may penetrate. It is a strong indictment of the Church that in its education it often produces such a non-evidential style of belief.

It is a serious charge, however, not only because of its social consequences, but because it contradicts what it is the Church's task to affirm. Such education is a subtle form of unbelief within the Church itself. It is a denial of the view that men are justified by faith, in favor of the view that they are justified by their opinions. Education in and by the Church has often, as a consequence, had damaging results.

It is not, however, the presence of the faith which creates a non-evidential style of belief; it is its absence. Those whose minds have been enchained by their education, are men of little faith. To say that men shall abide in faith does not mean they shall abide in their opinions, not even in their opinions about God. To think otherwise would be to suppose that God loves men because of their beliefs. There may be those who entertain such a faith, but it is surely not the kerygma that it has been the historic concern of the Church to affirm. The man of faith should be the most fearless in the search for truth because he knows that in the end it is not decisive. Being freed even from that most worldly of all concerns, namely the concern for his own salvation, he may be fearless even in his search for the truth about God.

One must add, however, that the Christian Church is not the only party in the modern world guilty of fostering a non-evidential style of belief. Our schools, including universities, have often been barbaric in the same way. Some years ago, in his studies on dogmatism, Rokeach and others tested many college freshmen in the east and middle west.[8] They were concerned to study the belief systems of these students, not only *what* they believed but *how* they believed it. The results were astonishing. The test included a series of statements accompanied by a series of reasons. The students were to indicate the statements and reasons with which they agreed. Remarkable numbers agreed with such statements as the following: "We ought to combat communism because communism means longer working hours and less pay," or "Hitler was wrong because otherwise he wouldn't have lost."

These are responses of persons who have been led to hold the "right beliefs" but never have been taught good reasons for them. There has

---

[8] Milton Rokeach and Albert Eglash, "A Scale for the Measurement of Intellectual Convictions," *Journal of Social Psychology*, XLIV (August, 1956), 135-141.

been learning which has resulted in the observable and verbal responses of the right kind, but for entirely erroneous reasons or for none at all except that such beliefs are "correct".

C. THE TOPOLOGY OF ENABLING BELIEFS

This emphasis on an evidential system of belief is susceptible to misunderstanding in a dangerous way. It could be understood to imply that one should not have *any* passionate convictions. A belief held evidentially is amenable to examination, and therefore open to change in the light of better reasons and more substantial evidence. Thus the possession of firm convictions seems to conflict with the cultivation of evidential beliefs. He who has passionate convictions is to that extent and at those points no longer open-minded, and he who is at *every* point open-minded must be without any passionate convictions. He is that completely flexible man, whose placid and weak mentality marks him off as dangerous, because he thinks nothing is really very important.

An evidential belief style does not commit us to such a mentality. The problem is rather to seek closure of mind at precisely those points and on those matters which will permit us to be open to the evidence on all other matters of belief. The only beliefs, in short, which must be rejected are those which prevent us from being open to reasons and evidence on all subsequent matters. As Chesterton has put it in another context: "There is a thought that stops thought. That is the only thought that ought to be stopped."[9] He might have added that there are beliefs without which no beliefs can be warranted and these are the only beliefs which at all cost must be affirmed.

Such beliefs, in fact, ought to enlist our most passionate loyalty, for they are the ones which enable us to hold all other beliefs in an evidential way. For example, a thorough skepticism in regard to reason, a kind of complete anti-intellectualism, if held to as a deep conviction, would successfully prevent the examination of any subsequent beliefs. It could lead only to a non-evidential way of believing. On the other hand, a "due regard for truth,"—the belief that truth is powerful, attainable and to be treasured whenever identified—such a belief is indispensable if *any* belief is to be held evidentially. Such a conviction does not commit us to the naive faith that all men have a due regard

---

[9] Gilbert K. Chesterton, *Orthodoxy* (New York: John Lane Co., 1909), p. 58.

for truth or are equally moved to dispassionately weigh and consider
the evidence on important questions. Nor does it commit us to the
truth of any specific belief. It commits us only to a certain *way* of holding beliefs, and that way is an evidential way. Indeed, a "due regard
for truth," understood in this way and passionately held to, is indispensable if we are to hold to *any* beliefs in an evidential way. A deep conviction concerning the value of truth is in this sense rationally defensible because without it there can be no rational defense of any belief
whatsoever.

It is not, therefore, the aim of teaching to eliminate all passionate
convictions. The aim, on the contrary, is to seek every possible assur-
ance that our passionate convictions, our enabling beliefs, are also rationally or evidentially held. Such enabling beliefs may be open for
examination, capable of refinement and elaboration, but under no
conditions can they be exchanged for others. Their abandonment cannot be warranted on the basis of evidence or reasons, because they are
precisely those beliefs without which we could not seriously entertain
the evidence.

These comments also are susceptible to a dangerous misappropria-
tion. At the point of enabling beliefs, there is only the most tenuous
line between the fanatic and men of less singular devotion. For at this
point, the difference between what is believed and how we belive it
is obscured. How a person believes something can be reduced, at this
point, to an account of what he believes. The actions of the inquisitor,
after all, may be defended on grounds of the most passionate regard
for truth, a regard for truth so strong, in fact, that it becomes necessary
to stamp out every trace of error that the truth may receive the recognition it deserves. The difficulty with the fanatic at every point, however, is that he confuses a due regard for truth with passionate concern
to propagate certain *specific truths.*

But it may be answered, "Is not a due regard for truth also a specific
set of beliefs?" It is indeed. It is the belief that truth is attainable,
powerful, and to be treasured. But the belief that truth is attainable
does not entail the belief that we have attained it. Such a regard for
truth does not permit us the illusion that we have appropriated more
than a fragmentary vision of the truth. It does not permit us with ease
to identify the truth. Rather, it places upon us the difficult and tortu-
ous task of weighing with great care whatever beliefs we may regard
as true, holding them always as open to challenge, and to change in
the light of further evidence and fresh reason. In short, although a

due regard for truth involves a passionate and unswerving loyalty to certain specific beliefs, although it involves a kind of fanaticism, it is an unyielding commitment to just those beliefs which will not permit the fanatic to develop.

It is at this point again that the Christian faith provides an interesting illustration. The Christian faith is often thought to be contained in certain doctrinal assertions. As such, it is commonly conceived to have more to do with *what* men believe than with *how* they believe. There is in this view a considerable burden of truth. But faith is not simply a matter of credal recitation; it is also a matter of fidelity. The fact is that *what* is believed in faith is precisely what is sufficient in order that all subsequent beliefs may be surveyed, examined, and held in an evidential way. What is believed, in short, has to do not so much with the beliefs we hold, as with the way we hold our beliefs. It has to do, in short, with the conditions without which we could not have a "due regard for truth," i.e., the conditions which permit us to develop an evidential "style of belief."

For example, one of the greatest barriers to a free and fearless search for truth is the tendency of men to identify their ideas with themselves, so that one cannot attack ideas without attacking their author. The result is that in debate beliefs are held non-evidentially, and reason is used in the fashion required by ideology, not as an instrument of inquiry, but as a weapon for defense of self. A "due regard for truth" then becomes extraordinarily difficult, and men find it virtually impossible to value the emergence of truth more highly than they value their own victory in debate. When we find such an attitude expressed in the practice of teaching, we recognize the authoritarian personality, the person who is less concerned that his words *be* truthful and more that they be regarded as the truth. Perhaps one ought to expect no more, for our beliefs are indispensable to ourselves; an attack upon them is an attack upon us.

This is, theologically speaking, the expression of man's unceasing effort to achieve salvation by works, to value his own ideas more highly than the truth, not because his thoughts carry a greater burden of truth, but simply because they are his. The man of faith is like any other man. He does not escape his condition, but along with others he may at least understand it, and understanding it place his hope elsewhere than in the fruits of his labor. For to walk in faith is to walk in the confidence that in death there is life, that beyond the death of self, there is hope for the freedom to think without any limitations except those imposed by the demands of thought itself. The quest for knowledge then holds no fears. Though it may displace one's ideas, it cannot endanger one's person. On the contrary, it can hold only inexhaustible surprises.

It is precisely the possibility of this kind of psychic freedom which lies at the heart of teaching. It is a due regard for truth which serves to distinguish the conversation of instruction from that of indoctrination. In indoctrination we are concerned primarily with *what* people believe and as a consequence are we concerned with *how* they believe it. In teaching, however, we are concerned primarily with *how* persons believe a thing and, therefore, can afford less concern with *what* they believe. If we adhere to the practice of teaching, we shall not be permitted a great anxiety over those who do not believe as we do, *provided* they can be led to a psychologically central regard for truth. For given that enabling belief, held with passionate conviction, it will follow that their beliefs, and our own as well, may be open to subsequent alteration in the face of reasons, evidence, and further reflection upon our experience. Apart from such beliefs, however, the hope that men's opinions may be changed by teaching is a hope in vain. Their beliefs will either be unalterable or else so easily changed as to fluctuate with every changing wind of doctrine or fashion of opinion. Without a due regard for truth, we must resort to indoctrination, force, or outright lies. With it, we may instruct. We may then say to men, in effect, "Come, let us reason together." A due regard for truth is an indispensable condition for that civilizing community in which not men but ideas are perpetually on trial.

Indoctrination, nonetheless, has a perfectly good and important role to play in education. There is nothing in these remarks which would suggest otherwise. Like the development of attitudes, indoctrination may be useful as the prelude to teaching. Just as we need not cut off the hand of every child or thrust one of every fifty into the street in order that they may understand the dangers of knives and highways, and learn to obey the rules established to protect their lives, so we need not offer reasons for every belief we think important for children and adults to hold. On the other hand, we have no warrant to inculcate beliefs for which there is no good reason, or for which we can offer no good reason, and we must be prepared to offer reasons or evidence when they are requested. Though indoctrination may, in many contexts, be both good and necessary, it can never be justified for its own sake. It can only be justified as the nearest approximation to teaching available at the moment. Indoctrination, in short, may be sanctioned only in order that beliefs adopted may later be redeemed by reasons, only that they may be vindicated by teaching.

D. TEACHING, LEARNING, AND EDUCATION

To say that indoctrination plays a legitimate role in education, but is, nonetheless, peripheral to the concept of teaching, is already to strike at an immensely important and powerful distinction. It is already to begin to describe the logical relations that exist between teaching and learning on the one hand, and teaching and education on the other.

Learning is commonly defined as any change of behavior. This definition, or one like it, has certain advantages for the science of psychology. It makes it possible to deal with learning as an observable phenomena, which is important if the study of learning is to remain a scientific inquiry. Such a definition, nonetheless, is wholly inadequate to capture what we normally mean by "learning". Ordinarily, we would regard a change of behavior at best as only *evidence* of learning, and we would not regard it as either necessary or sufficient evidence. A change of behavior in many contexts is not evidence that one has *learned* something new, but only that he has decided to *do* something new. A bank cashier who begins to embezzle, has not necessarily learned anything not learned by the cashier who does not embezzle. And this is so, because it is not obvious that learning to embezzle is distinguished in any way from simply learning to keep books. In this case, as in unnumbered others like it, a change of behavior is not sufficient evidence that anything new has been learned. But for exactly the same reasons it cannot be necessary evidence either. A person may learn to do something and yet never in his life decide to do it or in any other way display his knowledge or capacities. Unless such a supposition can be shown to be absurd or meaningless, it cannot be held that a change of behavior is a necessary part of what we *mean* by learning.

The important point to observe, however, is that regardless of our definition of learning, it must remain true that *every* point on the teaching continuum is *equally* a point of learning. Or, more precisely, every point on the teaching continuum, as much as any other, represents a method of bringing about learning. It is not therefore anything implicit in the concept of learning itself which distributes the teaching activities in certain logical relations along the teaching continuum.

They are distributed by the logic of the concept 'teaching' and not by the logic of the concept 'learning'. People can and will learn by propaganda, indoctrination, and lies. They can be brought to adopt certain patterns of behavior by conditioning, by intimidation, by deceit, by threats of physical violence. Indeed, these different methods appear on the teaching continuum *because* they are all ways of bringing about learning and because it is true *in some sense* that teaching aims at bringing about learning. It is not true, however, that every method of bringing about learning is equally a method of teaching. Some are more central to the concept of teaching than are others.

It is because of this logical fact that the teaching concept can yield a continuum of the kind I have described. It is an immensely important fact, however, that the concept of learning cannot yield such a continuum, and that it cannot for the following reasons. The concept of teaching includes within its limits a whole assemblage of human activities. Teaching stands related to instruction, training, indoctrination, and conditioning as genus to species. But it is not the relation between genus and species which is represented on the teaching continuum. Every point within the limits of teaching is a species of a certain genus, and *in this respect* no point is different from any other. The continuum, however, is directional; it is directional in a way that membership in a certain genus would not warrant. What is represented by the direction of the continuum is a logical relation between the *members* of the genus, indicating the extent to which they do or do not instantiate the properties of central importance in the logic of the concept. The concept of teaching is peculiar in the respect that not only does it stand related to certain activities as genus to species, but there is also between its species a discernable order.

If we consider learning to be a human activity, then it will also stand related to such things as drill, memorization, practice, and study, as genus to species. But among the species of learning there is *no* corresponding logical order of the kind that exists among activities of teaching. That is to say, the activities of learning fall under the concept as members of a class. It makes no sense to ask whether insight is more central logically to the concept of learning than, say, drill or practice or any other learning activity. But it *does* make sense to ask whether instruction is more central to the concept of teaching than, say, indoctrination. In short, teaching is a vague concept, but learning is not.

We might discover that some activities on the teaching continuum are more efficient or effective than others in bringing about learning, or that some methods of teaching are more appropriate to certain types of materials to be learned. But these distinctions cannot be discovered in the concept of learning itself. They must be discovered by empirical study. And such studies might show that the most effective methods of bringing about learning do not fall within the province of teaching at all. If that were to happen, it would follow that teachers ought *not* to adopt the most effective or efficient means of bringing about learning. In short, teaching and learning are conceptually independent *in the sense that* we cannot discover in the concept of learning, any principles sufficient to distinguish those kinds of learning aimed at in teaching from those which are not.

Now this may sound like an utterly fantastic and unwarranted claim, but it is not. Suppose it is true that by their consequences, we can identify many different kinds of learning. We can discriminate between learning habits and learning to obey certain principles, between acquiring belief sets and conditioned responses, or between learning by insight and by rote memorization. It is quite conceivable that different kinds of learning can be related to different points on the teaching continuum and, therefore, can be ordered in a certain relation to each other and some identified as more appropriate to teaching than others. For example, there may be a certain kind of learning which would result in a non-evidential belief set, and which might, therefore, be related to the methods of propaganda or indoctrination. Similarly, learning certain habits or skills might be related, more or less, to training or conditioning.[10] If this is so, then different kinds of learning can be placed in an order similar to the order of the teaching continuum. But the point is that this order is imposed upon the phenomena by the logic of the concept 'teaching'. There is no such order discoverable among species of learning. We can, in short, discriminate between kinds of learning and identify which are appropriately aimed at in teaching only if we *bring* to the concept of learning some principles or presuppositions which are derived from the concept of teaching. This is, in fact, what we usually do when we "select" from studies of learning those insights and truths which we think will be of practical use in classroom instruction. The fact remains that no species of learning is more centrally related to the con-

---

[10] I do not suppose there is in fact such a correspondence between kinds of learning and methods of enhancing learning. On the other hand, I see no logical reason why there should not be.

cept of learning than is any other. Therefore, when we discover how to bring about learning, it does not follow necessarily that we have discovered how to do anything we are concerned to do in teaching.

But what is the significance of this fact? The most immediate and far-reaching conclusion is a somewhat negative one. It is not clear within what limits or on what grounds we are warranted in deriving a theory of teaching from a theory of learning. To what extent, in other words, can our knowledge of learning be made to yield, in a logically defensible way, some principles which can be normative for the conduct of teaching? Indeed, one may ask whether there is any logically well-founded principle which will suffice to mediate the inference from the management of learning to the practice of teaching.

The problem arises because the concept of learning is of greater dimensions than the concept of teaching described in our topology. But the concept represented in that topology is the one we normally employ when we think about teaching in the setting of the school. How do we know then, that when we study certain phenomena of learning we are concerned with phenomena which fall within the more narrow limits of teaching? The fact is that apart from assumptions or presuppositions concerning the activity of teaching we do not know when our studies are relevant to the activity of teaching and when they are not. The methods of instruction and the techniques of deceit are both ways of inducing learning. On what possible grounds then, are we more concerned to master one than the other? Can it be that at this point we manifest a presupposition that one is in some sense more relevant to the practice of teaching than the other? On what grounds can we justify such a presupposition? Apart from some theory of teaching, assumptions of this kind have no warrant. Yet without such assumptions, we have no grounds for an inference from the principles of learning to the principles of teaching. In order to profit from our studies of learning, the logically prior problem is not to develop a general theory of learning, but to develop a theory of teaching. The topology of teaching described in these pages is a step in that direction.

There are, however, at least two other ways of meeting the logical problem posed by the conceptual relation between teaching and learning. The most attractive alternative is simply to extend the teaching concept so that it has a scope of equal dimensions with the concept of learning. Teaching understood in such an inclusive sense may be defined as any activity the primary purpose of which is to induce learning. Thus, the concept of teaching can be made to include within its limits all the endless activities which appear on the extended continuum, including the use of deceit, propaganda and outright lies. Such a move would suffice to guarantee that every discovery about the conduct of the learning process would have immediate and valid implications for the conduct of teaching. But the logical problem would not be solved. It would simply be made to appear at a different point. We would then have two concepts of teaching, a very inclusive sense and another more narrow sense. The problem then remains. Apart from some unexamined assumptions or presuppositions, we have no way of knowing when our knowledge of teaching in the wider sense is relevant to the conduct of teaching in the more restricted sense. We are left without any logical principle which will mediate the inference required.[11]

The second method of resolving this logical difficulty has to do less with the relation between teaching and learning and more with the relation between teaching and education. It may be argued that the construction of the teaching continuum is merely the consequence of certain social values which we share. It is because of our liberal-democratic tradition or because of our rational-humanistic inheritance that we do not regard the use of lies, propaganda and deceit as proper instruments of teaching. Apart from certain assumed values, it may be argued, any means of inducing learning, however barbarous they may seem to us, are perfectly bona fide methods of teaching. Thus, what we have been concerned with is not the difference between activities

---

[11] There is a third way of meeting this problem. It could be argued that the kinds of learning aimed at in teaching are only a special case of the wider phenomena of learning. Thus whatever one discovers about the process of inducing learning must *a fortiori* be true also of the activity of inducing learning by teaching. But what is the meaning of the phrase "special case of"? Does it point to a relation of class membership, class inclusion or to some other deductive relation?

Consider the following concepts and the relations of the members of the classes generated by each: (a) 'activities aimed at inducing learning', (b) 'activities aimed at inducing learning by teaching'. The class (b) is said to be a special case of (a) in the sense that $b<a$. Thus whatever is true of every member of the class (a) is true of every member of (b). But the class generated by (b) has a greater intension than the class whose members fall under (a). Thus the members of the class generated by (b) have certain properties *not* shared by other sub-sets falling under (a), and the problem is that in the present case, our concern is with exactly those features of the intension of the class (b) by virtue of which it is a sub-set of (a) and *not* those by virtue of which it is a "special case of" (a). Thus, it may be admitted that (b) is a "special case of" (a) in the sense that $b<a$. But this observation, though true, is not the kind of observation which will meet the difficulty posed by the relation between teaching and learning. What we need to study about the activity of teaching has to do with those respects which are not relevant to its being "a special case of" activities aimed at inducing learning.

of teaching on the one hand, and other methods of bringing about learning on the other hand. Instead, it may be argued that we have been concerned only to discriminate between good or socially sanctioned methods of teaching and bad or socially proscribed methods. In short, it might be held that the construction of the teaching continuum is possible only because of certain values which are presupposed in it and that all we require in the way of presuppositions about teaching is adequately provided by our commitment to these values.

This view, however, is fundamentally mistaken. The teaching continuum is in fact neutral as regards the different options of value from which men may choose. The relation between instruction and indoctrination, for example, has nothing to do with any presupposed values. The relation between them has been described on grounds of logic only. Between the activities of instructing and indoctrinating, there are certain striking resemblances. But there are also substantial differences. They are activities with different purposes. They aim at the development of different kinds of belief systems. They are differently related to a concern for truth. The process of each is differently related to the purpose of each. These relationships have nothing to do with the acceptance or rejection of any social values whatever. The logical relations will be the same whether we approve of indoctrination as a method of education or not. These distinctions will hold whether in our moral sentiments we are inclined to aristocracy, democracy or fascism. In this sense, the constructing of the teaching continuum does not rest upon any prior assumptions concerning what is valuable and what is not. All the difficult questions of values concerning the goals of education remain undecided and untouched by the topology of teaching. In this sense, such a topology is genuinely formal and neutral.

Moreover, the view that instruction is more centrally related to teaching than indoctrination has nothing to do with the relative value of one over the other or with our preference of one. It has to do simply with the fact that in so far as the conduct of indoctrination possesses certain properties, it resembles instruction, and as it lacks these properties, it resembles propaganda. And as this change occurs and indoctrination tends to assume the characteristics of propaganda, it becomes increasingly difficult to substitute the concept of "teaching" for the concept of "indoctrination" without a change in meaning. The topology of teaching therefore is not based upon any value presuppositions, but only on a series of logical distinctions.

From the topology of teaching it does follow, however, that education may be accomplished by other methods than teaching. In short, the idea of education, like the idea of learning, is of considerably larger dimensions than the idea of teaching. Education includes all of the enormously diverse means by which we learn, and these range all the way from the intricate processes of socialization to the rather formal methods of teaching mathematics and grammar. Propagandizing, lying, and intimidating are all methods we may use to educate. Education is therefore like an instrument. It can be used for any purpose men may adopt. It may be used to barbarize or to civilize. It may be used to liberate the heroic capacities of men and make them free or it may be used to make them cowards and slaves. Education is the kind of activity which may be adopted for many purposes. That is why the problem of value is important for educators. We must seek some grounds for determining what shall be our purposes. But though it is true that education can be used to accomplish many different purposes, it is not true that teaching is a method of education adequate to every purpose. One of the most difficult of all questions in educational theory is the question to what extent and within what limits shall we employ, or be permitted to employ, teaching as the method of education. In the construction of the teaching continuum, no resolution to these perpetual questions of value is presupposed. Education is an adequate instrument for barbarization, but teaching is not. Teaching is that human activity which is preeminently suited to enhance the human capacity for action. It is that activity of men which being engaged in, contains the conditions for the nurture of free human beings.

B. Paul Komisar
Temple University

V. TEACHING: ACT AND ENTERPRISE

A. INTRODUCTION

The pretext for this paper is to make a fresh run at resolving the controversy over whether learning is implicated in teaching. I say pretext, because for those not nourished by analytic ventures—and their number is legion, often the legion of the lugubrious—it is hoped that points made enroute to the main conclusion will be more fattening and, perhaps, bear more weight than the main argument. These apologetics notwithstanding, the central focus here will be on the question Does teaching imply learning? and the standard answer It does not. This answer is identified with B. O. Smith and Israel Scheffler, and I will refer to it as the standard thesis or the Smith-Scheffler thesis.[1] But a further point is needed. Though it is common to find the thesis stated in the casual way given above, one task is to make a casualty of this casual form of assertion. It is to be remembered that there is nothing that is teaching but that talking makes it so. Or to revert to the in-

---

Research for this paper was completed during a study leave granted to me by the Trustees of Temple University. I am grateful also to Gerald Reagan of Syracuse University for written comments on an earlier version of this paper presented to the Middle Atlantic States Philosophy of Education Society meeting in 1966. Finally, Thomas Nelson of Temple University severely edited the final draft, thus reducing what would have been my usually high number of errors.

[1] The standard thesis is to be found in Israel Scheffler, *The Language of Education* (Springfield, Ill.: Charles C Thomas, 1960), chs. 2 and 4; and B. O. Smith, "A Concept of Teaching," in *Language and Concepts of Education*, eds. Smith and R. H. Ennis (Chicago: Rand McNally, 1961), pp. 86-90. The thesis is affirmed by Frank W. Mitchell, "Some Notes on The Concept of Teaching," *The Journal of Teacher Education*, XVII (1966), 162-171; and firmed up by M. J. McCue Aschner, "Teaching, Learning and Mr. Gowin," *Studies in Philosophy and Education*, II (1962), 172-202, a response to D. B. Gowin (see below).

evitable jargon: the issue concerning the relation of teaching to learn-ing is a conceptual one, having to do with conditions for correctly ap-plying words and the implications to be drawn therefrom. We are not birdwatchers set out to directly espy things in nature.

The good that comes from this ghastly jargon is that it discourages us from proceeding as if there is a quite familiar and easily identifi-able activity we happen to call teaching. For on the assumption that there is, we are led to believe further that the nature of the bond be-tween teaching and learning is to be discovered by merely looking. This harnesses the donkey wrong-end forward. There is no activity that comes with the label 'teaching' attached to it in the way some moun-tains come topped with snow and some trees bear fruit. Right from the start our job is to determine whether a given performance that we are inclined to call teaching, that looks like teaching, and that others call teaching deserves the name. And more pointedly we want to know if the application of the name depends at all on the presence of learning among the students.

But it should not be imagined that this is merely an academic mat-ter. It is precisely when new cultural forms arise which are like yet unlike old forms, that we pause to study concepts grown stale with customs. So it is with 'teaching.' Like kitchen gadgets in housewifery, there are new devices in teaching which are not to be assimilated into traditional practices without a pondering of the premises of perform-ance. So this is a natural moment to ask about the features that are distinctive of teaching as customarily conceived. Then we can decide whether the computer and the film, the team and the machine require us to recalibrate our pedagogic concept. I will not be directly dealing with this larger issue. But it marks the general context in which this study is done.

B. SOME OBJECTIONS TO THE STANDARD THESIS

Considering the plainly conceptual nature of my task, it might seem surprising that there should be any debate at all. But a lively, though modestly sized, controversy has arisen over whether teaching implies learning.[2] It consists mostly of stating objections to the standard thesis

---

[2] For a sampler of the *published* forms of opposition and qualification, compare the fol-lowing: D. B. Gowin, "Teaching, Learning and Thirdness," *Studies in Philosophy and Education*, I (1961), 87-113; *idem*, ". . . Revisited," *ibid.*, II (1962), 287-298; Colin Camp-bell, "A Comment on Whether Teaching Implies Learning," *Harvard Educational Review*,

and making various attempts to overthrow it. If I may be allowed a conjecture, some of the critical reaction may spring from the passions aroused in those who read the Smith-Scheffler thesis as an attack on the once sacerdotal belief in the indivisibility of the teaching-learning process. As Harry Broudy once remarked, reference to the irrefragable unity of teaching and learning is "only a way of speaking because no educator really believes it to be true."[3] So talk about the bond of teaching and learning is gestural; it is the symbolic crux of an altogether worthy crusade to get teachers to feel pushed to look at the results of their teaching in the student. Educational talk not being notable for its precision, one can understand why the standard thesis is seen as worse than revisionism. But perhaps the thesis *is* treason and perhaps, also, this is the season for treason and the fit time for a countercampaign to release the teacher from preoccupation with learning. But the matter, as compelling as it is on its own account, is irrelevant to this part of the study. For taken in the clearest and most immediate way, as it is meant to be taken, the standard thesis says only that in a given instance we may truthfully report that someone is teaching X regardless of our state of knowledge of the student's learning of X. Now unless educators have gone mad and are incapable of literal, prosaic talk, it is on this simple literal level that the thesis should be debated.

Weakness of 'Circular' Stipulating

But even as literal doctrine, the Smith-Scheffler thesis has been opposed. A new meaning of teaching which implies learning is introduced by one line of opposition in a way that it is made part of the definition of the (consequently new) concept of teaching. A move of this kind might take this form: A dictinction between, say, instruction and teaching is introduced. Instruction is then defined *stipulatively* as any activity by a teacher done to produce learning. When the activity is successful, and the expected learning is achieved, then we can say the teacher was teaching, not merely (?) instructing. So much for that. Of course, any such move as the one depicted above has no effect on the standard thesis. Since that thesis incorporates a reportive definition

35 (1965), 82f.; John P. Powell, "Philosophical Models of Teaching," *Harvard Educational Review*, 35 (1965), 494-496; Elliot Eisner, "Instruction, Teaching, and Learning. . .", *Elementary School Journal*, 65 (1964), 115-119; [James E.] McClellan: review of Scheffler's "The Language of Education," in *The Journal of Philosophy*, LVIII, 15 (1961), 415-420.

3 Harry S. Broudy, *Building a Philosophy of Education* (Englewood Cliffs, N.J.: Prentice-Hall, Inc., 1961), p. 9.

(what a concept *does* mean), then no stipulative definition (what teaching *should* mean) can endanger it.

Indeed, what is the significance of attempts to change the meaning of the word teaching, so that learning is implied? If the stipulation is intended to avoid the thesis, it fails; it has no such consequence. If it is simply a proposal to educators to talk in a new way, then we have a right to ask why we should talk in this new way. One answer is that teaching would then imply learning. (And the slogan: No Learning, then No Teaching! would be a crisp rule of pedagogic language.) But one is hard pressed to imagine what possible advantage there is in a new meaning that requires us to ferret out the fact of student learning before we can say, with veracity, that a teacher is teaching. Therefore, one clear disadvantage of the proposal in my not altogether imaginary case is that, if it were adopted, we could speak of teaching only retrospectively.

Finally, and really more seriously, the stipulative formula "Let X mean Y (henceforth)" is no more than a part of the whole story of language change—and the easiest part at that. Who is going to work out the other intricate language adjustments that will ensue if X is allowed to mean Y? Language is too much a pattern of connections to fall before the mere voicing of a formula that isolates but one of its elements. We might take this as our policy: When someone (1) proposes a change in the meaning of a term, (2) works out a full account of the application of this newly defined term in all kinds of situations, (3) traces out the effects of the change on related terms, and (4) divulges the advantages and disadvantages of the new way of speaking, then and only then will we call this a stipulative definition and lend the stipulator our ear.

Reinforcement from Unexpected Quarters

Another type of venture to defeat the standard thesis takes several shapes, all unsuccessful. But the points raised are so plausible in their own right as to remove much of the sting from the standard thesis itself. Some critics are quite right in plumping for some special affinity between teaching and learning. It is not as if these were just *disparate* as, say 'teaching' and '1956 Chevrolet' are flat-out different.[4] The very solvent ring of 'Teaching does not imply learning' suggests some con-

---

[4] Unless it is used as wit, etc., for example directed to the teacher who wants his compensation in automobiles and has exaggerated the value of his services.

ceptual communion. Compare 'Teaching does not imply a 1956 Chevrolet,' which is too outrageous to honor with denial. What are these sharings? Well for one, both are human activities: a person can manage to teach and manage to learn, or one can fail at both, etc. So while not implicative terms, they are both from the same sector of the language, the human-doings sector. Also, while they do not have strict mutual implications, teaching carries with it a general *presumption* of learning produced. (But not the reverse; one would not presume in the presence of learning that its agency was teaching.) Learningless teaching must have to stop after a time, when it is chronic, when its absence is a thing of wonder. 'The teacher,' we say, 'owes us an explanation (i.e., justification).' So a common presumption of engaging in teaching is that it will, on the whole, produce some learning. If the learning continues to be absent, we don't *quite* say there has been no teaching, but it is a very, very near thing. At any rate, it's the kind of failure that immediately makes an accounting due, whereas a paucity in other desirable effects in the classroom—a bit of joy, a sense of wonder or respect for dignity in the student—carry no such levy.[5]

The presence or absence of learning, then, provides the occasion and *prima facie* grounds for evaluating some teaching or the teacher. But to say that *good* teaching leads to learning is irrelevant to the conceptual issue at stake here.

All these points may diminish the onslaught of the standard thesis on cherished pedagogical beliefs, but they detract not a whit from its literal correctness. We still say of Algernon at the midhour of a Friday morning, 'He is teaching,' regardless of whether his students are learning from him what he is teaching. But this is not a very onerous truth, and for certain purposes, as in the moral crusade alluded to earlier, we might exercise our eloquence in seeming contradiction to it or without appearing to notice it. And after all this is said, whatever remains disagreeable in the standard thesis can be avoided, I hope to show, not by denying the thesis but by so construing the concept of teaching as to render it innocuous. The further advantage of a flanking movement, as against direct assault on the standard thesis, is that it quickly exposes aspects of the concept of teaching which make the teaching-learning issue a paltry matter.

But the palliative has its price. The price in this case is a steady

---

[5] So we do not want to be thrown off the scent by that sense of 'implies' found in "The butler's actions imply guilt." For if learning be the crime, it is indeed the teacher's hand that is in the till; teachers at work strongly suggests learning is not far off.

diminution in the role of learning as the sole concern of teachers. So in the process of cutting into the dominion of the standard thesis, we come to give to learning its fitting place as only *one* desideratum in the activity called teaching.

C. LEVELS AND SENSES OF TEACHING

The focus in this paper is on the meaning of the concept of teaching and not on facts about the activity of teaching, such as, for example, that it is fatiguing work or only modestly paid. Let me begin then with the not entirely innocent move of positing three different levels at which talk of teaching occurs. (The term levels is not meant to carry serious implications; expressions such as sectors of use or areas of use would do just as well.) The levels are: the occupational, the enterprise, and the act. Each level of discourse, I argue, has its own distinctive sense of the term teaching.

Whether this move has significance, I will leave to the argument to show. But whether this move is possible can be decided forthwith by showing that the levels correspond to three types of variations on the question What is he doing?. The answer 'Teaching' is taken in a different sense at each level, as partly evidenced by divergencies in the set of what is excluded when 'He is teaching' is the correct answer. (I hasten to add that these garbled points are the topic for discussion below.)

Consider these variations on What is he doing?:

1) What is he doing (as work, for a living)?
2) What is he doing (now, on Tuesday morning, during this hour)?
3) What is he doing (asked by an observer about some particular phase of a lecture, discussion, or other classroom performance presently going on)?

The first thing to say is that 'Teaching' is an apt answer to each question, albeit presenting a new aspect in each case:

1) Teaching *names an occupation* or an activity habitually, characteristically engaged in.
2) Teaching *refers to a general enterprise*, some activity *being* engaged in.
3) Teaching *characterizes an act or alludes to an act as being of a certain sort* (belonging to a certain enterprise of teaching).

Levels and senses 1 and 2 are unexceptionable; everyone agrees we do use the word teaching to refer to an occupation and a general activity. Moreover, 'Frobisher is teaching,' said in the occupational sense does not require that Frobisher be engaged in the enterprise at the time of utterance. It only requires, for truth, that he is habitually so occupied, by contract perhaps (Frobisher teaches though at present he is taking his leisure under that tree.). This allowance is not made at the enterprise level nor at the act level. There, if he is truly teaching, then he is doing so now, when it is said. But to keep symmetry, being engaged in the enterprise doesn't require that one's act of the *moment* be a teaching act. It only requires that on the whole one will be doing such acts (He is teaching this hour, but at this instant he appears to be lining up the window shades.). One final comment: the word enterprise used at level 2 has no particular technical, much less a precise or rigorous, meaning; it is approximately synonymous with 'sequence of acts' or 'general activity' and the like. In truth, the term activity is more fitting for this level, but that term is already overburdened with controversy.

To return to polemical matters, the aptness of talk of teaching at the act level may strike some as open to challenge. I do not want to be taken as saying that 'Teaching' is the most specific or most informative answer that can be given in a typical context where a 3 question is asked. When, for example, there is no reason to be dubious about Zeno's performance, but an observer has blocked ears or has turned his back, then the observer, having regained perceptual functioning, might ask What is Zeno doing now?. The propitious answer would name some specific act, some specific way a topic is being treated: He is reporting the treaty conditions or He is reassuring the student. Here the answer is not 'Teaching' (it is assumed the whole enterprise is teaching in *that* sense), but some term more primly reportive of the action being taken.

Propriety of the Answer

But it is not always the case that teaching is a quasi-answer to 3. There are occasions when, though talk is at the act level, 'Teaching' is nonetheless the apt answer. Most pointedly it is so when 3 is asked after one observes a teacher engaged in such dubious practices as haranguing a student or perorating on a topic. *Then* the answer 'He has given off expressing his own prejudices and is finally teaching again' does the job smartly. It implies the previous act was not a teaching act. Or take another, this time a positive case: Teacher Cleon, new to his duties and eager to ingratiate himself with bureaucratic busybodies, begins his official activities with a shuffling two-step that in other circumstances might be considered charming. We, his friends, take this as a nonteaching act, attributable to nervousness but, we regret, not destined to be condoned on those grounds. But lo! The dance turns out to be a clever demonstration by which Cleon makes entry into a typical lesson. The act, we say happily, is one of teaching after all.

So the point of this is that there are acts that in certain circumstances can be aptly alluded to as 'acts of teaching.' By 'apt' here, I mean that the answer is as precise as it needs to be in view of the particular query being put; that is, it isn't just a very loose way of trying to report a specific type of act. Though redundant, the point might be put this way: When a question has to do with what act is being done, then the answer of 'Teaching' is evasive. But when the question asks how the act fits in, asks after the manner of the doing, then 'Teaching' is a proper answer.

Larger Scope of the Answer

There is another way, of not much bite, in which we talk about the act, yet speak in terms of teaching. Suppose someone mentioned such acts as showing, telling, proving, *et al.* and asked what general activities these could be acts of. The many possible answers could include 'acts of teaching.' So in an indirect way, talk of certain acts as teaching acts is defensible.

D. THE CONCEPT OF TEACHING AS CHARACTERISTICALLY ACCOMMODATING

Taking these considerations as thus far congenial, it can be said that there are three levels of teaching discourse. (Or: The concept of teaching is distributed over three linguistic domains.) I would be sorely vexed if this idea is interpreted as persuasive rather than reportive. We must face up to the fact that the concept of teaching is *characteristically accommodating*. On the one side it is wanton, allowing application of the term to the most bizarre performances when those performances are done in official circumstances: we see Teacher Cleon again in the presence of a properly constituted class during a scheduled class hour, lecturing at length to the walls and mumbling even then. It has to be admitted that Cleon is teaching (and not strolling on campus or advising in his office). Yet we must give sense too to the question Is Cleon really teaching?, when *real* has not the language innovating function attributed to it in the doctrine of persuasive definition, but rather signals a shift in levels of talk. Cleon is both teaching (and not exercising, as he might be doing at this hour) and not teaching (but talking to himself, though students happen to be present). That is, this represents a slip between two different levels of talk —in this case between enterprise and act—and the concept itself is pliant enough to allow this slippage. So it is the very application of the term, and not the caprice of this account, which allows for the looseness of enterprise reporting while yet retaining potential for more rigorous exclusion at the act level. Thus the term teaching belongs with other characteristically accommodating terms such as living and trying (What is he trying to do? and Is that really trying?).

E. CLARIFYING THE TEACHING ENTERPRISE

This feature of the concept of teaching, namely, that it is characteristically accommodating, sets the mark in trying to elucidate the concept. The goal is to arrive at a definition, or part of a definition, that succeeds in distinguishing teaching from those acts or activities that stand in contrast to it at the various levels. Some examples are:

1) If it is true that one is teaching as a life's work, then in a just world one is not a taxi-dancer by occupation or tolerating retirement.

2) At the enterprise level, the truth of 'Alec is teaching' excludes the truth of 'Alec is napping in the lounge' or 'Alec is promenading on the esplanade.'

3) Some contrasts with teaching at the act level are emoting, insinuating, deceiving, distorting, and expostulating when these acts are not for demonstration purposes.

One point—a bagatelle—about the meaning of teaching-as-occupation. It would not be untoward to define it in terms of standard institutional conditions and practices: to lecture, read and correct assignments, to be employed by a school or college, to be authorized to assign certain schooling tasks. This is the likely procedure for 'official teaching,' the occupation canonized by the Department of Labor and entered down in the official Book of Work. It will not quite do for *The*

One Who Teaches Children to be a Johnny Appleseed and dispense his largesse dutifully, but not as part of Official Duties. Here something in the content and manner of his intentions makes a person 'One Who Teaches.'

This brings us to the strategic difficulties that arise at the enterprise level. What is it that characterizes an 'enterprise' as teaching? To get an answer, it will help to make a rough division between two groups of activities that contrast with teaching at this level. First there is one rather assorted cluster of noninstructive activities (or *ceteris paribus* are presumed to be noninstructive). Included in the activities are the blatantly physical such as running sprints, the recreational ones such as driving to Pamona, the essentially introspective ones such as thinking about loss of faith. It is a bearable task to define the teaching enterprise so as to exclude these activities. And whatever problems arise are due probably to the abstract calling of the task as posed here; in context the demarcation should come easily. Given a concrete case, it is clear whether one is thinking about one's job as opposed to doing it. Though away from context whatever is offered as a sufficient difference can be challenged with those allowable cases where one does one's job by or through thinking about it (e.g., thinking about X in order to show learners something about thinking). Let me treat all such as special cases by admitting that almost any activity might be conducted for pedagogic purposes. But the justification for special case status is that their pedagogical use presupposes their standard nonpedagogical conduct. It would be pointless to do X as a demonstration unless there were standard (nondemonstrative) doings of X (not all golf swings are meant to teach or we would be teaching golf-swings-meant-to teach rather than golf swings).

Enough of aside. We can distinguish teaching from noninstructive activities by viewing teaching as an end-chasing performance and taking learning as the end being chased. I have no intention of disputing this answer. It treats of teaching as an activity not completely or always definable by content of performance (what is done) and thus takes care of the impasse quickly reached in the kind of definition given for teaching-as-occupation. And when teaching is partly defined as "an activity done with the *intent* to produce learning," we avoid the error, previously discussed, of supposing that the learning must actually result for one to be teaching. This is all part of the standard thesis, of course, and the thesis has the advantage of giving a criterion that sets off teaching from all noninstructive activities. So we can say of the golf pro, by way of defense, that he is not embracing the young lady, but teaching her to swing the driver. That is, his performance is part of a sequence meant to produce learning, not love.

But left on our hands is a second cluster of activities that *presumably* contrast with teaching. These I dub the 'cousined activities,' that is, cousins to teaching (and their names the 'cousined terms'). Included among the cousins are indoctrinating, training, propagandizing, preaching, haranguing, inspiriting, persuading, insinuating, deceiving, counseling, and moralizing.[6] Now precedent alone justifies the attempt to isolate teaching from these cousins; there is much literature in philosophy of education given over to this task with regard to indoctrination. But more than this, we must capture the point at issue in (what seems to be) the allowable charge: Zeno is moralizing (etc.) again, not teaching.

The special problem with these activities (and why I call them teaching cousins) is that they are done to change another's attitude or alter his character or have him adopt a new belief or new policy of action, etc., and all these intended changes can be called *learnings*. Hence the one criterion introduced earlier will not work to distinguish teaching from its cousins. But white water shows when we begin to look for another criterion. Roughly two kinds of criteria are tried. One is future-referring: Zeno is teaching (and not sermonizing) if the enterprise ends in not only learning, but learning that becomes suffused with reason (the teacher causes the light of understanding to glow in good time). The future reference can be disguised by stating the criterion as a special quality of the present intention. But saying that a teacher's intent to produce learning is unselfish and citing future reason in the learner's mind as attesting to the genuineness of the altruism all comes down to giving a future-referring criterion. And such a criterion fails from form alone, for it can not serve as a basis *now* for deciding whether Zeno is teaching. That such decisions are made and are not all predictions, I take as obvious. If more proof is necessary, suppose a student achieves the desired rationality following some classroom regimen. Then it would follow that whatever it was that happened in the classroom, it was teaching. Surely this is an unhappy

---

[6] These do not all contrast with teaching in the same way—if indeed some contrast at all. They constitute a mixed bag, albeit a bag whose contents need sorting out.

consequence. If obliteration overtook a class with a lesson just under-way, on a future-reference criterion others would be debarred from saying that the end came on a teaching note.

Ergo, any criterion will have to be stated as, or be reducible to, a criterion specifying some distinctive quality in present performance. The natural candidate for such an occurrent criterion is again drawn from canons of rationality: that one engages in the enterprise of teach-ing as one adheres to certain regulations of reasonable action. No one has given a full list of these regulations, but some are obvious, for example, citing evidence for facts, giving reasons for actions and recommended actions, allowing counter-theses to be voiced, and hon-oring objections with answers. But the flaw here is that rationality is not a distributing property in teaching, so the more scrupulously one adheres to the regulations, the more one makes a mockery of teaching (giving evidence for every statement, no matter how trivial; or allow-ing objections interminably). Nothing in the criterion stipulates or could stipulate the occasion for its application.

To round off this point, I claim failure in the project to distinguish teaching from its cousined activities; therefore at the enterprise level 'He is teaching' and 'He is training (etc.)' are not very different things (or at least we can not point with precision to how they differ). As a consequence, the sense of 'teaching' found in discourse at this level will not be the most distinctive or exclusive sense of the term.

The next move is to say much about the meaning of teaching at the act level. But it will serve the cause of criticism to mark this mid-point in the main argument by summarizing the whole of it. The argument runs as follows: Discounting occupational talk, teaching does not imply learning. This is the standard thesis and it is impec-cable. But this is true only at the enterprise level where the concept of teaching is *least* distinctive. The situation, I will go on to contend, reverses at the act level: here 'teaching' finds its most exclusive and precise meaning and, what is more surprising, here also use of the word *can* imply the achievement of teaching's endemic goal, albeit that goal is not learning. So to make short what is already stark, *as we become more strict regarding what is to count as teaching, the less likely it is that learning is the goal of the game, and the more likely it is that teaching implies the achievement of that which is the goal.* So much for where the argument goes; now to savor the getting there.

F. TEACHING ACTS

First the inevitable qualification. If one is of a mind to dissect the teaching enterprise, then allowable differences between schemes of classification result in divergent sets of rudimentary acts. This much is trite. So it is only out of convenience to this study, and not as the true classification, that the following set of teacher's acts is offered.[7]

a) Learning-Donor acts: acts intended to contribute rather directly and pointedly to the production of learning. Acts that appear to be of this kind are prompting, cueing, reinforcing, drilling, censuring or censoring, approving, showing, etc.

b) Learner-Enhancing acts: acts intended to put or maintain the learner in a fit state to receive instruction. Included among acts done to make the student 'learningable' are those intended to reduce anxiety, alleviate perceptual deficiencies, arouse interest, focus attention, and those often talked of as ego strengthening.

c) Intellectual acts (see below).

In addition it is possible that there might be separately identifiable performances of a content-arranging type, including things done to show or sustain sequence in the subject matter of an enterprise. However, I am not yet convinced enough of their generic status to chance them on a list. Finally, it is granted of course that mixed acts are possible, and likely abundant, in teaching.

The immediate point of this cursory listing is to introduce a restriction on the remaining discussion. The focus will be on intellectual acts. Thus there is no pretense that the final conclusion of this study holds for all teaching acts, except and insofar as such explicit claims are entered. In defense of this restriction, however, I make now, and defend later, the claim that intellectual acts have a very special status in teaching. Attention is not directed to peripheral matters. Still another prefatory point: I wish there were another term, less toxic to colleagues, to designate these acts. But *cognitive act* is no sweeter; *communicative act* and *interaction* are too unchaste, and, with regard to

---

[7] Cf. research reports by Arno Bellack, Ned Flanders, B. O. Smith, Hilda Taba, and others for some of these different classifications of teaching acts and even different conceptions of what a teaching act is.

the latter, jejune; and *logical act* gives a false connotation, as will be shown.

To begin serious discussion with another listing, here is a sample of intellectual acts:

introducing	proving	vindicating
demonstrating	characterizing	interpreting
citing	justifying	indicating
reporting	explicating	instancing
hypothesizing	defining	questioning
conjecturing	rating	elaborating
confirming	appraising	identifying
contrasting	amplifying	designating
explaining		comparing

(In the ensuing discussion I will often refer to these as teaching acts when the context makes it clear that it is teaching acts of the intellectual species being discussed.)

The task in this section is similar to the one faced in the preceding section: to determine what is meant in alluding to a given intellectual act as a teaching act. There is one difference however. Unlike the situation with regard to the enterprise level, at the act level we face a double charge: What is it that makes an intellectual act one of a certain kind, e.g., an act of justifying? And what further conditions are necessary to allude to it as (also) a teaching act. In the early part of the discussion these two steps will be treated as one. Only toward the end will the distinction be resurfaced and flaunted to clinch the closing step in the argument. Now to identify the defining characteristics, the criteria for intellectual acts of teaching.

Intent Is the Criterion

At act and enterprise levels the definitions of teaching are homocentric; they both use intentionality as the central defining element. But they go on to differ in that it is wrong to suppose that learning is what we intend to produce in the intellectual act, and it is niggardly to suppose that all such acts debouch in one type of outcome. With respect to the matter of learning as the goal of the performance, imagine that we go through the proof of some theorem (T) in such a way as to get an auditor to recognize it *as* a proof of T. It is extravagant to say that the intention is to produce learning of the proof of T. And it misperceives (by understating) what we do to say that the intention is just to get learning of T. For, if either is our intention, our performance would differ from the imagined case. If the intention is to learn the proof of T, we do not so much expose the reasoning (show irrelevant steps avoided, stress the argument, laud the elegance, etc.) as drill the students in the steps seriatim. In a word, we exercise rather than argue with the student. Likewise, if the intention is to induce learning of T as such—how T is worded or how to read it—once more as teachers, we employ a species of activity to achieve our intention, which differs from the imagined case. This suggests that the purpose in the original situation is most veraciously reported as 'intending to prove T to the student' or 'getting the student to grasp the proof.' No mention is made of learning in these statements.

One brief argument establishes the conclusion that learning is not what is intended in the intellectual act. In proving, demonstrating, elaborating, etc., we succeed in our aim even though the point grasped by the student may be promptly forgotten. *Learning*, however, is always dispositional. No intention to bring learning about is fulfilled unless there is a 'semi-lasting' effect on the student, by which I mean some presumption of reproducibility, however miniscule, beyond the immediate awareness. And this is a logical point about the *concept* of learning, not an empirical observation about the phenomena of learning. To put the same point differently: A teacher's claim to have reported a fact is not refuted on the ground that the student did not learn the fact (cannot later recall, repeat, reproduce it). The teacher can still assert truly that he did report the fact and treat the question But did the student learn it? as a matter for another day, a different time.

It will not do at this point to object that if all this about the nongoal of learning is true, then there is no difference between just giving a demonstration of X and demonstrating X so it is 'grasped' by the student. This objection seems to presume that in communication there are only two possible outcomes: either the auditor does not get the demonstration at all (as would be the case, e.g., if it were given in an alien tongue) or the auditor learns it. But there is at least one intervening stage (and probably more) between learning and nescience.[8] Lest how would we ensnare the difference between these two cases:

---

[8] Cf. Marcus Brown, "Knowing and Learning," *Harvard Educational Review*, 31 (1961), 125-144 for more on levels of learning; and the relevant discussion of the differences between teaching and telling in Israel Scheffler, *The Language of Education*, ch. 5.

a) Cleon introduces to some student the fact that the British government made overtures toward compromise with the American colonies prior to military conflict. The student was not aware of this before, and he gives sign of being so aware now by remarking on it. Nonetheless, on future occasions when it seems likely that one who knew or had learned the fact might cite it or show regard for its existence in other ways, the student does none of these things (no transfer).

b) Zeno is more successful or lucky. His student not only volunteers the information again and again (which might not impress the more demanding among us as learning), but seems influenced by the fact in whatever other ways Zeno demands as necessary for a claim of learning.

Now I say, of course, that there is a difference here and say further that a and b differ from the case where, following Cleon's efforts, still another student asks a classmate "What did he say? I didn't get it." and is destined never to be told.

Of course someone can always so construe 'learning' that nearly any effect at all is to be called learning. Under this interpretation students in both (a) and (b) learned, but one forgot or didn't transfer his learning. There is no way to refute such a counterclaim except to ask, seriously, not sarcastically, for the demonstrable advantages of a concept of learning which covers both a and b cases. Also we can ask how our old distinction between a and b is to be made in this new way of talk. For we do now have in the language we use in pedagogue-talk an oft-invoked way of distinguishing a from b: a is a case of awareness of X and b is a case of learning X. And the advantages of this distinction are patent.[9]

So in summary, the contention has been made that, with respect to teaching acts of the intellectual variety, learning is not what the teacher intends to produce. In showing flow on a flow-chart or movement of armies on a map, the intention is to point up perception and not learn the habit of it. In guiding students to a solution of a problem, the teacher's aim is to have students figure out the solution, not 'learn the figuring out.' And in explaining an event, the goal is an auditor who comprehends the event, not 'learns the comprehension.' And so

---

[9] For one instance from empirical research where the distinction between learning and awareness is salient, see D. D. Merrill, "Learning a Hierarchical Task," *Journal of Educational Psychology*, 56 (1956), 225-234.

if we catch Zeno in the midst of elaborating on a thesis and ask him what he is trying to get the students to learn, Zeno might tell us what the whole enterprise is after, or he could say Nothing, I'm just trying to show how this thesis develops. And the latter answer is not impertinence.

The other claim made at the beginning of this section was that there was no single, universal intention called learning in acts of teaching. It strikes me that variety, rather than uniformity, characterizes act goals. Unfortunately, and despite seasonal promises to redeem the language of educational objectives, we lack in education a crisp, orderly, and uniform vocabulary for reporting goals at the intellectual act level.[10] But even in resorting to what natural language has to offer, the variety is striking: it is intended that the student get the point, grasp the idea, come to the solution, become aware of connections, see the larger view, and such.

But the point about variety is not one to be strict about. If we *must* have a single expression to impose unity on these outcomes, then the best I can draw from a deprived imagination is *awareness*. It doesn't cover very well the differences between, for example, seeing a solution and perceiving a fact, but it makes a brief final summary statement possible: *It is not some kind of learning, but some form of awareness, which is the intended upshot in the teaching acts under discussion.*

Uniqueness of Intellectual Teaching Acts

The contrast between act and enterprise continues into the kind of performance done to carry out the intention at each level. In the abstract it is easy enough to say this difference is that intellectual teaching acts are logically lucid, whereas this need not be true of the teaching enterprise on a whole nor true of other acts within it.[11] But to say what logical lucidity is and especially to show what it is not are more arduous tasks for a variety of causes. Generally, though not too clearly, intellectual acts are logically lucid in that the act is done not only with the intention of securing a certain 'uptake' (an awareness of some point), but also so as (a) to divulge to the student what the intention is and (b) to achieve his awareness by identifying the

---

[10] Which may not be all bad. The area has not yet been delineated by the educationist but neither has it been devastated by him!

[11] The notion of logical lucidity is freely adapted from H. P. Grice, "Meaning," *Philosophical Review*, LXVII (1957), 377-388; and P. F. Strawson, "Intention and Convention in Speech Acts," *Philosophical Review*, LXXIV (1964), 439-466.

reasons given as the intelligible grounds for the point the students are to become aware of. Finally, neither *a* nor *b* is essential to the overall enterprise of teaching (or other teaching acts).

This covers the differentia all right, but there is a clear need for embellishment. So to illustrate the criterion of lucidity in at least one context, once more consult Frobisher, who is engaged, as is his wont, in demonstrating to a class the operation of some infernal machine. Frobisher intends the students to become aware that the machine works in certain ways. If this intention is not already apparent to the students, Frobisher makes it so. (A constant perplexity in a study of the kind undertaken in this paper is how much clarification to give assorted claims. The clarification usually resides in things teachers do and say, such trite and quite mundane things that one hesitates to mention them. But in the present instance, by 'divulging the intention' I mean such familiar classroom utterances as What I want you to see is . . . or The point of this is . . . , etc.) In the course of accomplishing his intention, Frobisher engages in sundry doings, showings, and sayings. It is to be understood that in these doings and sayings Frobisher is avowedly *giving* the students the grounds for taking the machine as operating in the manner indicated.

There are various ways of stating the point at issue in the illustration: Telling the student how the machine works and demonstrating the machine's workings are the same or are intrinsically related. Or, in still another argot, the teaching act is one in which the material, efficient, and formal causes of a result are all part and the same part of the act executed to yield the result.

Enumerable qualifications await offstage, but the intellectual act features are seen more sharply through contrast with situations in which they are absent. First, and least plausibly, Frobisher's real intention might be to evoke in his class an acute desire to own such machines and to persuade others to buy them. (Frobisher on the edge of indigency has bought up the only company producing them. Demand, never great, has declined, and he has a hearty supply to hand.) Frobisher might go through the same account he would give if his intention were pedagogically honorable (if he knew the students were particularly ready to go from perception to action), but what makes this case artificial is that given his secret self-serving design, Frobisher's labors will likely carry him beyond the familiar regimen. And he will soon supply us with an illustration of a second sort of act failure, this one of more pedagogic verisimilitude. Frobisher now has a more salubrious intention and seems to go through a typical performance. From the student's viewpoint, however, and perhaps from Frobisher's viewpoint as well, what brings the student around to view the operation as indicated, is not the official performance but the allusive cues, asides, crafty looks, and tenuous threats accompanying (and indeed parodying) the more visible agenda. By these devices the students are persuaded that *not* to take the awareness as officially avowed would brook peril.

Thus in invoking the criterion of logical lucidity we place intellectual acts in opposition to acts of influencing, deceiving, training, and those other 'cousins to teaching' that have act counterparts and which we were so desirous to exclude from teaching, but could not, at the enterprise level. For the class of acts under scrutiny does *not* include cases where:

a) The causes, but not the reasons, for awareness are displayed. (Students are convincingly praised for taking X as explaining Y, but not given the grounds for same.)
b) Not the grounds themselves (though they may be given), but something in the manner or circumstances of presenting them is meant to elicit awareness. (Students accept X as an instance of Y, because of the authority or prestige of the teacher doing the presenting, though this is not meant to include the cases where a legitimate *and intended* ground for a point is the teacher's authority.)
c) The end sought is clearly not the end avowed. (A point is said to be offered as tentative, but is treated dogmatically.)

So here at the act level we avoid thorns that ever snagged us in connection with the teaching enterprise. The act is lucid when *all* conditions for genuine 'uptake' are revealed or are tacit for the entire act, whereas it could not be true of the whole of the enterprise in which the act is featured.

All of this adds up to support for the cause espoused in this paper. A way has been found to give the concept of teaching an exclusive sense by distinguishing it from various cousined terms. And this exclusivity applies only at the act level of talk, which itself constitutes half the case for my final conclusion. But before proceeding from this point to the remaining moves of the argument, a brief interlude is in order. For as soon as the point is made that lucidity lends distinction to the intellectual act, it needs hedging in so many ways as to perhaps vitiate it. Nevertheless, since the hedges stand as asides to the main argument, short shrift will be their fate.

First, since 'act-uptakes' are marked by variety, it follows that what counts as satisfying the criterion of lucidity will vary enormously from act to act. In elaborating on an idea, what count as grounds for taking the result as bona fide elaboration (and not, say, reduction or refutation) are not the same as the reasons one gives to make auditors aware that X explains Z or that X justifies Z.

Second, though in discussion thus far I glibly referred to the teacher as divulging *reasons* to the auditor, it is important not to confuse the grounds we give students for taking X as the case with the official backing for X being the case. When we speak of reasons for X, it is usually in the sense of official backing for X being the case. But students are not always fitted out to receive the considerations that on public occasions among knowledgeable adults we cite to attest to the truth or whatever of propositions.

It is hoped, of course, that over time and at propitious moments in the course of education students are proficient, and there can be isomorphism between the reasons for X being the case and grounds teachers present to students for taking X as so. But this is not typical, else what would education be for? So teachers naturally adjust presentations to the auditors' ability, their stage of development, and the significance of the content being taught. Hence we get the problem of intelligibility discussed in educational theory. Various devices are suggested for conflating reasons and grounds in pedagogic bliss, and theories are contrived to tell how and why to do this. But the problem of intelligibility can be ignored here. My concern is with the criterion of lucidity itself, and this criterion says nothing about *what* grounds should be given.

Finally, the simple statement of the criterion given heretofore exaggerates it in two unimportant ways:

a) It is not suggested that the teacher, to be teaching, must be the one who does and says everything. The teacher may arrange for others to make some or all of the moves and yet they can be the *teacher's* acts of teaching. Otherwise teaching would imply lecturing, which it clearly does not (despite appearances). But one thing *is* implied when we say a teacher is justifying, etc.: it is the teacher who sanctions, authorizes, censors what is stated or done by others. It is implicit in the very concept of teaching, I take it, that the teacher passes on the admissibility or inadmissibilty of act-related content. So anyone can speak the words or do the showing, but the teacher can not execute a policy of intellectual laissez-faire and maintain that the act-description is teaching. But even the admissibility function can be variously, even indirectly, performed, but none of this need detain us further.

b) Nor does the criterion of lucidity require that all the grounds must be *said*. Some can be tacit. But the tacit grounds must be sayable, compatible with what is or could be said (and would be said), if the assumption of implicit recognition is correct. (In demonstrating a machine, it is tacit that at any given time we are naming or talking about the thing being pointed to. If this convention happens not to be followed by the auditor, then it is a candidate for 'the said.')

Enough hedging. I would hold, still, that this criterion sets off the teaching enterprise and other teaching acts from those acts that are intellectual. None of this comes to denying that there are some acts that have a comparable lucidity. One such is the teacher-directed exercise, or drill, to go by its name in the trade. Here a teacher exhibits that it is learning, and not comprehending or seeing the point, that is the aim. A certain procedure is laid on; the student is enjoined to perform it again and again, with as much variation as logistic imagination allows; and the students are heartened in this practice by announcements that "Practice makes perfect" or some such, which, given the state of the pedagogic art, justifies to the student in a sincere way that the means are suitable to the end of getting learning. So here we have a nonintellectual teaching act (an instance of what was earlier called a 'learning-donor' act) which possesses something like the lucidity found in intellectual acts.

Examine whole sequences of acts and you find the same happy occasions when the teacher is able to flaunt the aim (Today we are to learn about penguins.) and lets slip something of the grounds, i.e., the rationale for the learning-inducing procedures being emulated. But, I argue, these must be felicitous and not defining instances. No proof can be offered to support this claim, but there are considerations to be cited in its behalf. Schools, for example, make all manner of arrangements to promote learning, but these arrangements are such that they could not in the normal turn of events be divulged to the student as part of the very procedures undertaken to promote the learning.[12] Presumably the large 'institutional steps' we take in the conduct of the general enterprise of teaching are based on knowledge and experience the student is being initiated into. Thus the student would have to be well along in his education for its conduct to be plausible. The preclusion is not a logical impossibility, but just a discomfiting fact, a sad matter of human psychology that we cannot give to the one who is learning a full disclosure of how the learning is being made to come about. Nonetheless, a presumption that one can do this gives purport to periodic proposals to teach the young the learning theories (or whatever) their education is supposedly based on. But if the enterprise of teaching were already patently lucid these proposals would be jejune. (Imagine a suggestion that we should teach the student what 'illustration' means in the act of illustrating.) It's the unwelcome fact that the teaching enterprise lacks intelligibility, more or less, which gives point to the idea of teaching learning theory; it's the pedagogue's way of squirming before his destiny.

In consequence, as the institution of education becomes more scientific, more rationalized, then the dissimilarity between the logical lucidity of the act and the logical obscurity of the enterprise will be more pronounced. For what makes some teaching enterprises partly lucid now is that they follow common sense maxims about learning which even the child absorbs early. But as education becomes more scientifically based (genuinely, that is, not just avowed), it will be less lucid to the student (and less like teaching).

So the point of this section is that intellectual teaching acts are unique in that their performance requires a logical lucidity that may be found in enterprises and other acts, but only by happenstance.

Requisites of a Teaching Performance

The plot of this long story becomes clearer; a twist or two and it stands exposed. The impression may have been gained that any intellectual act is *ipso facto* a teaching act. The impression is wrong. The acts of

---

[12] I would add, though more timorously, that the same is true even of the aim itself. It is to be doubted that the aim of the teacher can be divulged to the student forthrightly. True, one hears jolly talk about the desirability of teachers exposing their hands to the student. But what exactly can the teacher do other than to utter certain words. The utterances are possible, but what meaning can they have to students who are being *initiated* into decimals, marginal utility, energy levels, or whatever. Such aims must lack something in the way of intelligibility for them. Indeed for some of the 'higher' appreciations, nearly a whole way of life needs to be absorbed before one is even aware of what scientific method or critical thinking or literary appreciation can *mean*.

justifying, instancing, etc., are in a special way fungible; they can be as much a part of arguing, book writing, conversing, debating, and disseminating as a part of teaching. So the last move in this argument is to show the final features, which if present make a teaching performance out of an intellectual act.

There are two such features. The first carries much freight of its own but not as part of this study. The second brings the main argument to its ordained end.

a) For the performance of an intellectual act to count as teaching, assorted conditions must obtain which make the act possible. Thus the act of designating an object presupposes a distinguishable object to so designate. One is not engaged in reporting anything to an auditor who is unable to comprehend the language used—nor can the inexplicable be explained. This class of conditions is a welter, containing as it does things having to do with the state of the subject matter as well as the proficiencies of teacher and auditor. I'll not attempt to tidy it up any more than to note that the teacher is committed to putting and keeping the learner in a 'perceiving-and-learning-able' state, and rendering the subject matter 'teaching-competent.'

b) More pertinently, to dub intellectual performances as teaching acts signals that the act verbs (i.e., *to demonstrate, to prove,* etc.) are being used in their auditor sense. These verbs tend to have dual uses. One can, for example, give the introduction to a topic without introducing that topic *to* someone; we can offer justification for a policy which doesn't succeed in justifying the policy to a particular audience; or we can give instances of a general idea, yet not be illustrating the idea for someone. Thus the important distinction made by Roland and Bomberger between explanation and explaining-something-to-someone needs to be generalized to cover all intellectual act verbs.[13] It is as if these verbs took either a conventional context or a social (interactive) one. One can explain X by citing those propositions that count as 'giving an explanation,' regardless of the presence or absence of an audience (The explanation for the fiscal crisis is in chapter seven.). But in the sense of 'explaining something to someone,' the conventional aspect is modulated by having to achieve a certain 'uptake' in the other person. And it is very much the case that the moves

---

[13] S. Bomberger, "An Approach to Explanation," *Analytical Philosophy*, Second Series, edited by R. J. Butler (New York: Barnes & Noble, 1965), pp. 2-105. Jane Roland, "Explaining, Understanding and Teaching History: A Philosophical Analysis" (Ph.D. diss., Harvard University, 1961), ch. 3-4.

made, the things said and cited will vary with the needs and state of the auditor.

This consideration that intellectual acts count as teaching acts only in their auditor sense has a consequence that writes finis to my brief. For it follows that success in performing the act requires success in bringing about the appropriate kind of awareness (exception noted in next section). The teacher cannot be successfully introducing a topic to a student without its being the case that the student is being introduced to it. One *can* successfully give the proof of a thesis (in the midst of arguing or writing) without getting 'uptake' from the disputants, discussants, or readers. Furthermore, the argument can be won with that proof, though the proof be unacceptable to, or even missed by, the other party. But not so when the intellectual acts are to count as teaching. Exemplifying an idea for a student requires that the student requires that the student comes to recognize something as illustrating the idea.

Since this is the decisive point in the argument, allow for its iteration: *As regards acts like demonstrating, proving, etc., in order to be doing them at all, an auditor is required, who is successfully becoming aware of the point of the act.* This denies the idea that there are two stages: first the teacher is *demonstrating* something, and then when the student gets the point, the teacher is *demonstrating successfully.* There are not two stages. Rather the claim is that 'auditor-uptake' is a precondition of the doing of the act itself. So one can not say 'I see you are explaining X to John, but is John understanding X?' If you *are* explaining to John, then John is getting it. The idea of doing as separate from succeeding does not enter here; *doing is succeeding.*[14]

Of course in connection with these acts, one can speak of trying as against succeeding. But the trying is 'trying to explain' and *not* 'explaining and trying to get understanding.' Notice, please, that the opposite holds true of conventional nonauditor intellectual acts, where we can say 'I gave the proof of T, hoping John would grasp it, but he didn't.' So in the case of nonauditor-directed acts, trying can apply in two ways: one can try to give the proof and fail to give it (too many interruptions); or one can give the proof all right, as part of trying to get student awareness, yet fail to get the awareness (student too inattentive). Yet the latter case is recorded in the Angel's Archives as 'giving the proof.' All this nicely sets off 'proving T to someone' from 'giving the proof of T.'

---

[14] It is in this sense that the means-ends model can be said to be inappropriate to teaching acts. The teacher's act of explaining is not a *means* to the *end* of student understanding.

The consequence for my brief is that, while teaching in the enterprise sense may not imply learning, the auditor-directed (teaching) acts do entail the achievement of their endemic goals (awareness). So Zeno can say 'I am teaching him about the course of Spanish conquest' without implying learning. But if Zeno is instancing moments of success in the Spanish conquest, then Zeno's auditor *is* becoming aware of the instances.

None of this is meant to attribute Promethean powers to teachers, but simply to take note of a logical feature present when some act verbs correctly characterize what teachers do. The point is a small one, not overladen with immediate practical significance. But whatever import the point has, it is due to the presence of the preposition (T is demonstrated *to* John)—one case where the preposition carries the import.

Significance of the Auditor

A certain ambiguity clutches the conclusion just arrived at. Hence this last section is added, by way of anticlimax, to quell incipient refutation. In seeming contradiction to what I have been saying, it does appear that:

a) Intellectual acts of the nonauditor variety can also be taken as teaching acts.
b) When these are teaching acts they do not entail auditor awareness.
c) These nonauditor acts are teaching acts, because and only because they are part of a teaching enterprise.
d) Therefore, whenever any acts, including ones directed by the auditors, are dubbed teaching acts, it is because of their place in the overall enterprise of teaching.

The first three statements are true but trifling; the last, which harms my case, is just false. Concerning the first three, take the case of a proof given in such a way as to be described as 'giving the proof' rather than 'proving T to Student Smith.' The circumstances in which it can be a teaching act are those encountered earlier in connection with Zeno's shuffling dance, where we said after suitable prologue, Zeno is teaching after all. The evidence leading up to such an admission is that the act in question partakes of some larger teaching enterprise, some sequence of acts done to induce learning. In that derivative sense, nonauditor intellectual acts—any act indeed—can be called a teaching act.

Now an objector might want to parlay this admission into a general criticism of my whole strategy of distinguishing act from enterprise. The objection can be imagined to run as follows:

> Yes, it is true that we can talk of teaching at the act level; or with reference to a particular act, ask whether someone is teaching. But in doing so, can it be said that we are restricting our attention solely to the act? Isn't it the case of saying that the act is one of teaching only as it partakes of a larger activity, which we *first* take to be teaching? If so, then there is no separate act level or act sense of teaching. It's just the enterprise sense once more (with its attendant difficulties)—only now we focus on a segment of the enterprise. Thus, to talk at the act level is not the same as talking to (just) the act. And the act is not the referent of the utterance, but only the occasion for it.

The objection is justified at this point, because, in the earlier discussion of the reasons for assuming an 'act-enterprise' distinction, I left one point untended—putting it off for the relevant moment. The objector's case is granted for all acts *except the class of intellectual ones directed to the auditor.* And this is why I have taken pains to niche them separately. The peculiar thing about such acts (in addition to features already covered) is that such acts can be called teaching without allusion to any particular sequence in which they occur. We do this catholically in such assertions as 'In order to argue with him at all, I had to teach him the difference between validity and truth' and 'We didn't enjoy the conversation but I taught him, at least, to keep to the point' and more tellingly yet, 'I doubt it will have any effect, but I did teach him that virtue is patient.' Here teaching has the sense of 'making aware,' not 'inducing learning' (note the last utterance); the acts belong to no teaching enterprise; and it is the constituent reality *of the act itself* which makes the term teaching appropriate. Ergo, we talk not only *at* the act level, but refer solely *to* the act.

Lastly, this very special use of *teaching* has a distinctiveness and exclusivity not found in looser talk about 'learning-inducing' activities, and *their* derivative acts. Indeed, to think of the teaching enterprise as somehow primal and every other sense of teaching as derivative is to get the matter reversed. The strictest, the basic, the keenest concept of teaching we have is the concept we apply to designate particular occurrences of intellectual acts directed to the auditor. Let the study of teaching begin there.

R. S. Peters
University of London

VI. MUST AN EDUCATOR HAVE AN AIM?

Many in recent times have blamed philosophers for neglecting their traditional task in relation to education. For, in the old days, it is argued, philosophers explained what the good life and the good society were; and this provided aims for educationists. But nowadays, as Sir Richard Livingstone put it, we are lacking in a knowledge of the 'science of good and evil'. I think that most modern philosophers would claim that, in this respect, they had advisedly neglected their traditional task, for the very good reason that they have become clearer about what their task as philosophers is. The so-called 'revolution in philosophy' of the twentieth century has been largely a matter of becoming clearer about what philosophy is and is not. And one of the conclusions that has emerged is that it is not a sort of super-science of good and evil.

However, this newly found modesty about providing blueprints for the good life does not altogether either excuse or explain the neglect by modern philosophers of philosophical problems connected with education. I do not think that this neglect springs from the conviction that there *are* no such philosophical problems. Rather it is because philosophers have been so concerned with their 'revolution' that they have concentrated more on the central problems of philosophy—those connected with knowledge and belief, appearance and reality, free will and determinism, mind and body, space and time. Peripheral problems connected with concepts like 'education', 'authority', and

Reprinted from R. S. Peters, *Authority, Responsibility, and Education,* rev. ed. (London: George Allen & Unwin, 1963), Ch. 7.

'character' have been crowded out, as Hobbes put it, 'no otherwise than the sun deprives the rest of the stars of light, not by hindering their action, but by obscuring and hiding them with his excess of brightness'. It is time that philosophers supplemented their sun worship by a bit of star-gazing—but this, as I shall try to show, does not mean trying to return to the old task of constructing a horoscope of educational aims.

I suppose the conviction that an educator must have aims is generated by the concept of 'education' itself; for it is a concept that has a standard or norm, as it were, built into it. To speak of 'education', even in contexts quite remote from that of the class-room, is to commit oneself, by implication, to a judgment of value. One might say, for instance, that it was a 'real education' for compilers of the Wolfenden Report to wander round Piccadilly at night-time. Some state of mind is here presupposed which is regarded as commendable, and some particular experiences are regarded as leading on to or contributing to it. There is thus a wide sense of 'education' in which almost anything could be regarded as being part of one's education. Rousseau said that 'education comes to us from nature, from men, and from things'. And of course he was right; for the concept works in as wide a way as this. But there is a narrower and more usual sense of 'education' in which *men* are very much to the fore. For we usually speak of education in contexts where we consciously put ourselves or others in such improving situations.

Given that 'education' implies, first, some commendable state of mind and, secondly, some experience that is thought to lead up to or to contribute to it, and given also that people are usually deliberately put in the way of such experiences, it is only too easy to think of the whole business in terms of models like those of building a bridge or going on a journey. The commendable state of mind is thought of as an end to be aimed at, and the experiences which lead up to it are regarded as means to its attainment. For this model of adopting means to premeditated ends is one that haunts all our thinking about the promotion of what is valuable. In the educational sphere we therefore tend to look round for the equivalent of bridges to be built or ports to be steered to. Hence the complaints of lack of direction when obvious candidates do not appear to fill the bill.

It is my conviction that this model misleads us in the sphere of education. We have got the wrong picture of the way in which values must enter into education; this is what occasions the disillusioned muttering about the absence of agreed aims. But to bring out how we are misled we must look at the contexts where the means-end model *is* appropriate. There is, first of all, that of plans and purposes where we do things in order to put ourselves in the way of other things. We get on a bus in order to get to work; we fill up a form in order to get some spectacles. Our life is not just doing one thing after another; we impose plans and schedules on what we do by treating some as instrumental to others. Some of these we regard as more commendable than others, and what we call our scale of values bears witness to such choices. The second means-end context is that of making or producing things. We mix the flour in order to make a cake or weld steel in order to make a bridge. We speak of the end-product in a factory and of the means of production in an economic system.

In both these contexts we might well ask a person what he was aiming at, what his objective was. But in both cases the answer would usually be in terms of something pretty concrete. He might say something like 'getting a better job' or 'marrying the girl' in the first context; or something like 'producing a soundless aeroplane' in the second. Similarly if a teacher was asked what he was aiming at, he might state a limited objective like 'getting at least six children through the eleven-plus'. But he might, as it were, lift his eyes a bit from the scene of battle and commit himself to one of the more general aims of education—elusive things like 'the self-realization of the individual', 'character', 'wisdom', or 'citizenship'. But here the trouble starts: for going to school is not a *means* to these in the way in which getting on a bus is a means to getting to work; and they are not made or produced out of the material of the mind in the way in which a penny is produced out of copper. These very general aims are neither goals nor are they end-products. Like 'happiness' they are high-sounding ways of talking about doing some things rather than others and doing them in a certain manner.

It might be objected that education is an art like medicine and that in medicine there is a commonly accepted end-product—physical health. Why should there not be a similar one for education—mental health, for instance? The answer is fairly obvious. Doctors deal mainly with the body and if they agree about what constitutes physical health it is because it can be defined in terms of physical criteria like temperature level and metabolism rate. Also there is little objection to manipulating and tinkering with the body in order to bring about the required result.

In the case of education, however, there are no agreed criteria for defining mental health; for either it designates something purely negative like the absence of unconscious conflicts, or, in so far as it is a positive concept, it has highly disputable personal and social preferences written into it. Also education is not, like medicine or psychiatry, a remedial business. When we are concerned with the minds of men there are objections to bringing about positive results in certain sorts of ways. People make moral objections to prefrontal leucotomy even as a remedial measure. How much more objectionable would it be to promote some more positive state of mind, like a love of peace, in all men by giving them drugs or operating on everyone at birth? Indeed, in my view, disputes between educationists, which take the form of disputes about aims, have largely been disputes about the desirability of a variety of principles involved in such procedures. Values are involved in education not so much as goals or end-products, but as principles implicit in different manners of proceeding or producing.

Of course there can be considerable disagreement about the value of what is to be passed on as well as about the manner of passing it on. At the moment, for instance, there is much disagreement as to whether education should be liberal, technical, or vocational. And this reflects different assessments about the value of what is to be passed on, which is a matter of governmental policies as well as of personal preferences. An educator has an important social function in a community and, however idiosyncratic his individual aims may be, he cannot be completely indifferent to the pressing needs of the community, especially if he is paid by the state. Different weight is attached by different educators to the needs of the community as distinct from those of the individual child. Indeed those who stress 'mental health' as an educational aim may well be protesting against the effects of collective pressure on the individual. Instead of trying to interpret this aim positively we might regard it as a timely warning against pushing the individual into socially approved tasks at too great a cost to his stability. It is as if a teacher was insisting that, whilst he was fulfilling his essential social function of passing on information and skills and preparing children for different jobs, it should never be forgotten that children may become unhappy and neurotic, isolates from their group, or sexually unbalanced. And the educator should not disregard these other things that go to make up 'the whole man.' In the old days talk of 'character-training' used to serve as a corrective to undue academic or vocational pressure, or religious ideals were appealed to. But nowadays such a corrective must seem to have scientific authority. So 'mental health' enters the field of education—the old Aristotelian 'harmony of the soul' in respectable trappings.

But those who stress the importance of a 'liberal' education are not merely voicing a protest against an academic or vocational emphasis in education which neglects the individual needs of children. Neither are they claiming merely that there should be arts subjects in the curriculum as well as science and typewriting. Their protest relates to the manner as well as to the matter of education. For both science and arts subjects can be passed on by liberal or illiberal procedures. Literature and science can both be treated as 'subjects' and, as it were, stamped in to a student. Or they can be treated as living disciplines of critical thought and of the imagination, in which the student can be trained on an apprenticeship system. 'Liberal' is a term used of certain types of principles and procedures such as respect for persons and facts, toleration, and deciding matters by discussion rather than by dictat. Its association with the *content* of courses is derivative from the belief that some subjects foster such principles more than others. But this is a naïve view—rather like the strange belief that technical colleges can be made more 'liberal' if a certain amount of time is devoted to teaching 'the humanities' to supplement science subjects. For it is surely the *manner* in which any course is presented rather than its matter which is crucial in developing a liberal attitude of mind.

To illustrate more clearly the distinction which I am drawing between 'aims' and 'principles of procedure', let me take a parallel from politics. A man who believes in equality, might, like Godwin, be lured by a positive picture of a society in which differences between people would be minimized. He might want to get rid of differences in wealth and rank, even to breed people in the attempt to iron out innate differences. He might even go so far as to advocate the abolition of institutions like the army or the Church in which some men were given opportunities of lording it over others. Another social reformer, however, might employ the principle of equality in a much more negative sense without any concrete picture to lure him on his journey. He might insist, merely, that whatever social changes were introduced, no one should be treated differently from anyone else unless a good reason could be produced to justify such unequal treatment. The Godwin type of man would rightly be regarded as pursuing equality as a very general aim; the more cautious Liberal would have no particular aim connected with equality. He would merely insist that whatever schemes were put forward must not be introduced in a way which would infringe his procedural principle.

I think that this is an illuminating parallel to the point I am trying to make about the aims of education. For, in my view, many disputes about the aims of education are disputes about principles of procedure rather than about 'aims' in the sense of objectives to be arrived at by taking appropriate means. The so-called 'aims' in part pick out the different valuations which are built into the different procedures like training, conditioning, the use of authority, teaching by example and rational explanation, all of which fall under the general concept of 'education'.

Consider, for instance, the classic dispute about the aims of education which is so often connected with an argument about the derivation of the word 'education'. There were those like Sir Percy Nunn who stressed the connection with *educere*—to lead out. For them the aim of education must therefore be the development or realization of individual potentialities. Others, like Sir John Adams, stressed the derivation from *educare*—to train, or mould according to some specification. They might be regarded as people who in fact believed in aims in a proper sense, in moulding boys into Christian gentlemen, for instance. The progressive who protests against this conception of education is not simply jibbing at the end-product of a Christian gentleman. He is also jibbing at the assimilation of education to an art where something is produced out of material. Rousseau, for instance, protested vociferously against treating children as little mannikins, as material to be poured into an adult mould. A child, he argued, should be treated with respect as a person. The progressive, therefore, like Dewey or Kilpatrick, presents another picture of the educational process. The child's interest must be awakened and he must be put into situations where the task rather than the man exerts the discipline. He will thus acquire habits and skills that are useful to him, and, by co-operating with others in common tasks, will develop respect for others and for himself. In the eyes of the progressive the use of authority as a principle of procedure is not only an inefficient way to pass on skills and information; it is also an immoral way to treat a child. It is made even worse in both respects by techniques like the use of reward and punishment.

So at the one end of the family tree generated by the concept of 'education' there are procedures involving the use of authority in which the voice and the cane are used to produce a desirable end-product. Education is here thought of after the model of means to ends in the arts. At the other end the model of purpose and planning is stressed; but it is the purpose and planning of the child, not of the adult. As Rousseau put it: 'By attempting nothing in the beginning you would have produced an educational prodigy.'

But, as any educationist must know, if he reflects on the matter, these are only a limited selection of the procedures that are in fact employed. There is, for instance, the influence exerted by one person on another in some sort of apprenticeship system, when the teacher guides rather than goads. We learn carpentry by doing it with some-one who is a bit better at carpentry; we learn to think clearly by talking with someone who thinks a bit more clearly than we do. And this other person need not be a charismatic figure so beloved by the advocates of 'impressionism' in the public schools or Boy Scout movement. It may be a person who is not only skilled but who has the additional ability of being able to explain and give an account of what he is up to. Progressives often object to talk and chalk and confuse the use of the voice with one way in which it is used—the authoritative way. But most good teachers use their voices to excite and to explain, not simply to instruct, command, or drill.

My guess is that most of the important things in education are passed on in this manner—by example and explanation. An attitude, a skill, is caught; sensitivity, a critical mind, respect for people and facts develop where an articulate and intelligent exponent is on the job. Yet the model of means to ends is not remotely applicable to the transaction that is taking place. Values, of course, are involved in the transaction; if they were not it would not be called 'education'. Yet they are not end-products or terminating points of the process. They reside both in the skills and cultural traditions that are passed on and in the procedure for passing them on. As Aristotle put the matter long ago:

> For the things we have to learn before we can do them, we learn by doing them, e.g. men become builders by building, and lyre-players by playing the lyre; so too we become just by doing just acts, temperate

by doing temperate acts . . . but it is not the man who does these that is just and temperate, but the man who does them *as* just and temperate men do them.

And how can this happen unless we learn them in the company of experienced practitioners who understand what they are doing and who can explain it to others?

There are all sorts of things that can be passed on that are valuable. Almost anything, as I started off by saying, can be regarded as being of educational value. And, to a large extent, those who favour one type of procedure rather than another choose examples that suit themselves and advocate the practice of things that can be passed on best in accordance with their favourite model. The man who advocates authority and drill is most at home with things like Latin and arithmetic where rules have simply to be learnt defining what is right or wrong and where, in the early stages at any rate, there is little scope for rational explanation or learning by experience. The progressive is most at home with things like art, drama, and environmental studies where projects can develop without too much artificiality. And the man who believes in rational instruction is usually inclined towards things like science, history, and geometry. An intelligent teacher, I suppose, will always first try to interest his pupils. As Whitehead put it, romance must precede precision. But, given the interest, he will adapt his procedure to what he is trying to teach.

In society generally there are those who are prone to view life not as a stream of experience to be enjoyed nor as a series of predicaments to be lived through but as a chain of obstacles to be overcome in the pursuit of goals that stretch out like a chain of oases in a desert, or as recalcitrant material to be moulded into some pleasing social or personal pattern. And, of course, many of the things which we do can be regarded as ways of implementing concrete and limited objectives. But this picture of the pursuit of aims is often exalted into grandiose talk about the purpose of life or the purpose of political activity. Self-realization, the greatest happiness of the greatest number, and the classless society act as lures to provide a distant destination for the great journey of life.

Such general aims are not just harmless extravagances due to the overworking of a limited model of means to ends, a sort of metaphysical whistle in the dark. For men will do terrible things to other men in order to implement aims like racial purity which are both idiotic and illusory. The crucial question to ask, when men wax enthusiastic on the subject of their aims, is what *procedures* are to be adopted in order to implement them. We then get down to moral brass tacks. Do they in fact favour the model of implementing aims taken from the arts and from technology? There are those who favour the maximum of authoritative regulation such as is necessary in an army; there are those who use other people and mould them for their own purposes; there are those who are determined to live according to rational principles and to extend the maximum of toleration to others who disagree with them; there are those whose preoccupation is the pursuit of private good for whom hell is the other fellow.

These differences of procedure are writ large in the family, in economic affairs, and in political life. In education they are accentuated because the impact of man upon man is more conscious and because people are put into positions of authority where there is great scope for adopting their favoured procedures. My point is that arguments about the aims of education reflect these basic differences in principles of procedure. The Puritan and the Catholic both thought they were promoting God's kingdom, but they thought it had to be promoted in a different manner. And the different manner made it quite a different kingdom.

Of course arguments about general aims do not reflect *only* differences in principles of procedure or disagreements about the relative importance of public needs and individual development. Equally important are valuations of content where the merits of, e.g. art as distinct from those of science or history are under discussion. But the real issues involved in such comparisons are obscured by talk about self-realization, life, happiness, and so on. For what sort of self is to be realized? What quality of life is worth perpetuating? Teachers surely care whether or not poetry rather than push-pin is perpetuated, to use a time-honoured example. The problem of justifying such 'higher' activities is one of the most difficult and persistent problems in ethics. But talk about self-realization and other such omnibus 'ends' does more than obscure it; it also encourages an *instrumental* way of looking at the problem of justification. For a nebulous end is invented which such activities are supposed to lead up to, because it is erroneously assumed that education must be justified by reference to an end which is extrinsic to it. The truth is much more that there is a quality of life embedded in the activities which constitute education, and that 'self-realization' can be explicated only by reference to such activities. Thus, if by 'life' is meant what goes on outside schools and universities, there is an important sense in which 'life' must be for the sake of education, not education for life.

Author's Note: This lecture was given about ten years ago and has occasioned many misunderstandings, e.g., that the author thinks educators should never state their aims, that aims necessarily pick out procedures, and that there is no place in education for planning means to ends. It would require another lecture to remove such misunderstandings in a way that is consistent with the main thesis advanced in this lecture. If the reader is interested in following up such points he should consult the author's more recent writings on the topic—especially *Ethics and Education* (London: Allen and Unwin, 1966), chs. 1 and 2; and "Aims of Education—A Conceptual Inquiry" in *Philosophy and Education: Proceedings of the International Seminar* (The Ontario Institute for Studies in Education, Monograph Series No. 3, 1967).

Dwayne Huebner
Teachers College
Columbia University

VII. CURRICULUM AS A FIELD OF STUDY

I should like to offer four propositions, upon which this discussion of curriculum will be based:

1. Current conceptions of curriculum are inadequate in that they tie the educative process only to the world of man's technique and exclude ties to the world of his spirit.
2. This inadequacy stems from an overdependency upon a conception of value as goals or objectives, and a consequent overdependency upon learning as the major characteristic of man's temporality.
3. This inadequacy can be partially corrected by a conception of curriculum as the design of an educative environment in which valued educational activity can occur.
4. This designing is inherently a political process by means of which the curricular worker seeks to attain a just environment. . . .

In 1832 Oswald Spengler's pessimistic *Man and Technic* was published in English. He argued that man's Viking quality, his search for power, has resulted in the establishment of a machine technic which is in the process of destroying man, and that it is now beyond man's power to alter this destiny. He states:

> The lord of the World is becoming the slave of the Machine, which is forcing him—forcing us all whether we are aware of it or not—to follow its course. . . .

Reprinted with the permission of the publisher from Helen F. Robinson's *Precedents and Promise in the Curriculum Field* (New York: Teachers College Press), © 1966, Teachers College, Columbia University.

> All things organic are dying in the grip of organization. An artificial world is permeating and poisoning the natural. . . .
>
> The history of this technics is fast drawing to its inevitable close. . . . Faced as we are with this destiny, there is only one world-outlook that is worthy of us, that which has already been mentioned as the choice of Achilles—better a short life, full of deeds and glory, than a long life without content. Already the danger is so great, for every individual, every class, every people, that to cherish any illusion whatever is deplorable . . . . Only dreamers believe that there is a way out. Optimism is cowardice.[1]

In 1964 Jacques Ellul's *The Technological Society*,[2] originally published in the 1950's in France, was translated into English. Ellul spelled out the danger more incisively. He defined technique not simply as machine, but as "the totality of methods rationally arrived at and having absolute efficiency (for a given stage of development) in every field of human endeavor." Technique permeates not simply the machine world, but the economic, political, and social structures of man's world. He points out that the two most commonly accepted characteristics of technique are its rationality and artificiality. But more significant are five other characteristics less widely acknowledged. First, its automatism:

> When everything has been measured and calculated mathematically so that the method which has been decided upon is satisfactory from the rational point of view, and when, from the practical point of view, the method is manifestly the most efficient of all those hitherto employed or those in competition with it, then the movement becomes self-directing . . . . [Then] man is stripped of his faculty of choice and he is satisfied.[3]

Second, its self-augmentation, the "automatic growth of everything which concerns technique." Here man has lost control of the growth of technique, as Spengler pointed out, or as McLuhan writes, "Man becomes, as it were, the sex organs of the machine."[4] Ellul states that "technical progress is irreversible" and that it tends to a geometric, not an arithmetic progression. It poses primarily technical problems which can only be resolved by technique and thus becomes a closed world.

---

[1] Oswald Spengler, *Man and Technic*, translated by Charles Francis Atkinson (New York: Alfred A. Knopf, 1932), pp. 90-104.

[2] Jacques Ellul, *The Technological Society*, translated by John Wilkinson (New York: Alfred A. Knopf, 1964).

[3] *Ibid.*, pp. 79-82.

[4] Marshall McLuhan, *Understanding Media: The Extensions of Man* (New York: Mc-Graw-Hill, 1964), p. 46.

Its third characteristic is its monism. "The technical phenomena, embracing all separate techniques forms a whole." Its fourth is its universalism; it "cannot be otherwise than totalitarian," and it "has taken over the whole of civilization." Technique tends to expand geographically, into all parts of the world; and qualitatively, into all of men's endeavors.

Finally, technique is autonomous, a closed system, an end in itself. "The complete separation of the goal from the mechanism, the limitation of the problem to the means, and the refusal to interfere in any way with efficiency," all of this "lies at the basis of technical autonomy."

Ellul, in the book just mentioned, seems to share Spengler's pessimism. However, in a more recent article he suggests conditions which might lead to a solution of the problems posed by the autonomy of techniques.[5] It is relatively easy to hypothesize that the recent concern for instructional technology or instructional systems is but the result of technique's universalism reaching into the world of the school. This would, however, be mis-stating the case. For one thing such a view lends itself to a rejection of modern technologies in schools, as if the classroom were the last bastion of naturalness and humanness and consequently must be protected from the encroachments of this monster, technique. In fact, it would seem that technical developments point to what man is and what he can be as much as the arts. Whether we like what is pointed out is another question. To reject technological developments in classrooms is to reject part of man and to deny the evolution of new possibilities in man. If there is any place in our society where the struggle between the world of man's technique and the world of man's spirit should occur, it is the classroom. It is here that men should discover how to make technique serve man rather than man serve technique. It is in the classroom where the neotechnic civilization that Mumford[6] talks about should be aborning, for where else should man's spirit be uppermost?

The other things wrong with the hypothesis are that the universalism of technique first touched schools when the clock (which Mumford claims is the first technical development) was installed on the

[5] Jacques Ellul, "The Technological Order," in Carl F. Stover (Ed.), *The Technological Order* (Detroit: Wayne State University Press, 1963), pp. 10-37. (This is a resumé of Ellul's earlier book.)

[6] Lewis Mumford, *Technique and Civilization* (New York: Harcourt, Brace and World, 1934).

classroom wall; that technique achieved a firmer grip when the first mass medium, the book, was used; and that education really embraced technique when it became concerned about efficiency before the 1920's.[7]

The invasion of the schools by technique is not symbolized by modern developments in electronic instructional technology. Technique is already firmly, although perhaps not permanently, institutionalized in the means-ends language which guides the educational process. What is the first great question which focuses most of the debate in education? "What is the role of the school?" or "What are the purposes of education?" What question do we try to get beginning teachers to ask as they plan? "What are your purposes?" "What are you trying to achieve?" "What is it that you want students to learn?" And the next question, which presumably can be answered only after the first—"How should the school be organized to achieve that end" "How should your content and instruction be structured to get there?" Left unsung, but nevertheless in the back of everyone's mind is the criterion of efficiency. Whatever and however you organize, do so efficiently. Conceived that way, the machines and the new technologies are merely more efficient ways to reach goals. This is unfortunate. New educational technologies do increase educational efficiency through their quality as means. But new developments in educational media also suggest new values that could be achieved through education. This value-creating quality is hidden when new media are seen simply as means to ends.

Most educators seem unaware of their involvement with and commitment and subservience to the self-augmenting technological order. Their curriculum language hides this reality from them. In fact, it also hides how new technologies could be used to sharpen the struggle between man's techniques and man's spirit. The unfortunate equating of education with learning has pushed into ascendency theories of learning[8] and has justified the means-ends value system which is characteristic of technique. Focusing on learning as the primary working concept in curriculum will naturally push the educator to ask, "Well, what are they supposed to learn?" When these goals or expected out-

---

[7] Lee Raymond Callahan, *Education and the Cult of Efficiency* (Chicago: The University of Chicago Press, 1962).

[8] For another criticism of the dominance of education by psychology see Joseph J. Schwab, "On the Corruption of Education by Psychology," *The School Review, 67*, Summer, 1958, pp. 169-184.

comes are specified, then the learning theory supposedly tells the teacher how to use materials and what to do. The search is for the most effective means to realize the ends. Hence curriculum people search for the best materials, the most efficient organization, and the best grouping of children. Let me remind you again of Ellul's definition of technique: "the totality of methods rationally arrived at and having absolute efficiency (for a given stage of development) in every field of human endeavor." Learning theory is, thus, the handmaiden of technique in the schools. It subjects teacher, materials, and organization to the system. Theoretically, it prescribes the means and tells teachers and students how to act.

Do not misunderstand me, I am not against learning theories. As a language system in psychology, they exhibit man's transcendent spirit, his ability to reach out into the unknown. They are essential for the evolution of education. One of the major contributions of learning theory to education is to facilitate the construction of the educational environment. In one sense, it might be said that learning theory has finally found its limited and proper place in curriculum as it makes possible teaching machines, programmed learning, and electronic, responsive environments such as that of Omar K. Moore.[9] Through the insights of reinforcement theory, those miserable old workbooks are being improved and may yet become functional in schools. Furthermore, through the development of many such environmental objects, the teacher is becoming a free agent again, for one of the characteristics of the older classroom technologies was that teachers became extensions of the technique. Builders of textbook series would describe in detail how a teacher should use the textbook. In effect, they were saying, "Here is the reality, the book. Now your role, teacher, is to become the active ingredient in this technology. How you feel is unimportant, for you are but an extension of the book and its purposes." The moment there is more than one technique available for the classroom, the teacher enters the realm of freedom and awesome choice. However, to the extent that learning theories become the sole sources of the educator's ideology, they bind the educational process into the technical order.

The problem, if not caused by the equating of education and learn-

---

[9] For the promises of learning theory in the design of the educational environment, see Robert Glaser (Ed.), *Teaching Machines and Programmed Learning, II, Data and Directions* (Washington: Department of Audio-Visual Instruction, National Education Association, 1965).

ing, is at least epitomized by it. The difficulty is that man's spirit is much more complicated than we seem willing to believe. Oversimplified educational ideologies foster this misconception. The goal-oriented, person-shaping ideology of curriculum implies that youngsters can be molded to reach predetermined behaviors. The educational process is more complicated than that. The act of education is an act of human influence—or of "initiation," as Peters would say[10]—and there is nothing more complicated or awesome. The school is the meeting ground of a man becoming aware that he has a destiny and a social group seeking to determine that destiny. It is this idea of destiny that curriculum thought has destroyed by making learning the most important single concept in its language repertoire. In a sense, destiny has been replaced by destination, and learning has become the only valued form of living in school.

Man's nature is given by his temporality—the fact that he lives in time as well as in space. If this age of rapid change has done nothing else, it has disclosed that man is the being capable of continual modification and change. When the world was rather stable, at least over a twenty- or thirty-year period, the educator could well envision a state of man with more or less permanent and fixed characteristics. He could imagine a perfect gentleman, an ideal citizen, or a skilled artisan, and he could program a curriculum accordingly. Today this is impossible, for change outside of man is too rapid. This is exciting and revealing, for it points so clearly to the fact that man is embodied change. Not only can he produce change, but he himself is capable of continual change. To be a man is to be capable of finite change and evolution until death. Indeed, the insight of the existentialists seems relevant, that man's biography may be written, his project complete, only after he is dead. A living man may always become something else; if he doesn't of his own accord, the world may push him into it. How do we deal with this in education? The standard answer is, "by helping people learn how to learn." I think this answer is inadequate, for it hides the question or the problem within existing categories; whereas the existing categories need to be upset, maybe even destroyed, so new questions and problems can emerge. Rather, it seems that this awareness of the significance of change deals the death blow to the concept of learning as central in curriculum thought. It is still necessary, for

---

[10] R. S. Peters, "Education as Initiation," in Reginald D. Archambault (Ed.), *Philosophical Analysis and Education* (London: Routledge and Kegan Paul, 1965), pp. 87-111.

it is an instrumental category for fabricating an educational environment. But I do not believe that it can continue to be the central category of curriculum thought. Learning is an attachment, a fixation, a state of conditionedness; while man's essence is given by the antinomies of attachment and detachment, fixation and freedom, conditionedness and unconditionedness. Learning implies a determining of behavior, while man's reactions in the world are partially indeterminate. Learning implies a destination; whereas living as a man implies a destiny. In some ways the discussions about creativity a few years ago pointed to this conflict, for the educator, between the determinateness of learned behavior and the freedom essential for creative behavior. And, of course, one is not possible without the other. But when learning remains the central concept in curriculum, we tend to focus on only one side of man's ambiguous situation in this world.

The basic problem is finding a way to conceptualize man's durational quality—the fact that man's existence is a temporal existence. It has continuity, it extends into the past and into the future. It could almost be said that man is a "human becoming" rather than a human being, but to say so is to throw overboard the philosophical heritage which deals with the nature of being. It might be said that man's home is not space but time (hence the significance of history as the foundation of all realms of life and knowledge). The educator has had difficulty dealing with the temporal quality of man, which is one of the reasons he has latched onto the behavioral scientist's notions of learning and goal or objective. To conceive of behavior as goal-oriented is to bring to one level of awareness this durational quality. Learning is that process which occurs between the identification and the attainment of the goal. The problem arises when there is no goal. What happens then? Does life have no durational quality? Unfortunately one branch of the publishing field has destroyed the significance of the words, but time is life and vice versa. To waste time is not to waste a commodity, it is to waste one's life. To kill time is to say that life during those moments is of no significance and that the person might as well be dead. Time wasted in classrooms is an almost unforgivable crime because it is life and the precious eternal moment that are really being wasted.

But the behavioral scientist, upon whom the educator has become too dependent, has trouble dealing with the temporal qualities of existence. He tends to spatialize life, to assume that time as a dimension has the same qualities as space, and to forget the irreversibility and unpredictable qualities of man's temporality. Hannah Arendt indicates that these qualities require the power to forgive and to promise in social life.[11] Developmental psychologists, such as Gesell, introduce the notion of stage; the person jumps from stage to stage. An observer readily sees the stages but has difficulty seeing the process of movement between stages. The curriculum worker has the same difficulty. He identifies concepts or attitudes or skills that are to be developed, and the student goes from one level of skill or concept to another. Again, then, the time inbetween is conceptualized as learning. The curriculum specialist has trouble thinking of the inbetween times as life with inherent value—these times are simply pathways to ends. Of course, the curriculum worker and his cohort, the behavioral scientist, have tried to get away from this by discussion of processes: the knowledge-making process, the problem-solving process, the discovery process, and the creative process. But each of these also has an end which is used to identify the consequences of the process. It is unfortunate that the educator has neglected other fields of insight, for the philosopher, the artist, and the theologian all have dealt with man as a temporal being.[12]

Closely related to this conceptual problem of dealing with man's temporality is the problem of value in curriculum. The educator's major approach to value is that of an end to be achieved, an instrumental type of valuing. Constantly the questions are asked, "What are we trying to achieve?" "What are the goals of education?" "What is our purpose?" "How well will this device or textbook series accomplish our goals?" The problem of value is the most significant one faced by the curriculum worker. Unfortunately, most discussions of the problem are subsumed under this heading of purpose or objectives. The problem of value is closely tied to the processes of criticism. It is frequently through acts of criticism that implicit values are made explicit (art criticism) or that the need for new values is realized (social criticism). The major source of educational criticism internal to the educational process is evaluation. Almost the sole criterion for measuring the value of a school or curriculum is "How well were the goals achieved?" As the conceptual model of learning is thought by some to

---

[11] Hannah Arendt, *The Human Condition* (Chicago: University of Chicago Press, 1958).

[12] Henri Bergson, *An Introduction to Metaphysics*, translated by T. E. Helmo (New York: Liberal Arts Press, 1949); Martin Heidegger, *Being and Time*, translated by John Macquerrie and Edward Robinson (New York: Harper and Row, 1962); Joseph Campbell (Ed.), *Man and Time*, papers from the Erenos Yearbooks (Baltimore: The Johns Hopkins Press, 1956).

provide a model for teaching, so the conceptual model for evaluation is thought by most to be the model for curriculum planning. The existing model for evaluation, technically conceived, is fine and very productive. As a model for curriculum, the evaluation model is inadequate. Furthermore, evaluation is not the only form of valuing which may be brought to bear on educational processes. It could well be that the failure to provide other valuing procedures, or preferably, other forms of criticism, has led to the desire for a national testing program. It is so easy to criticize on the basis of ends achieved or not achieved, for this requires no discipline except for the instrument maker. To use other forms of criticism in the search for other values requires much more skill and knowledge.

Let me recapitulate the discussion so far. I have proposed that current ways of thinking about curriculum are inadequate because they tie the teacher and the student to the self-augmenting world of technique. This invasion of the schools by technique is not the result of our use of new instruments or technologies of instruction, but a result of our basic means-ends approach to education. This means-ends approach is typified most directly by our uncritical acceptance of learning as our key working concept, and by the conception of value as an end state to be reached. As long as educational values are conceptualized only as goals to be reached or behaviors to be learned, the classrooms will continue to serve man's technique rather than man's spirit.

If the means-ends model (goals to be achieved and learning theory as the way) is relegated to a subordinate position in curricular thought, then how can the curriculum specialist proceed?[13] First, he needs a way of thinking about man's existence in time and the phenomenon of change. If all of man's behavior in the educative process need not be conceptualized as learning, how else may it be designated? This becomes the problem of finding a way to talk about educational activity, for it is educational activity which must be uppermost in our thinking, not simply learning activity. The central notion for the curriculum specialist must be that of educational activity, a term which cur-

[13] See R. S. Peters, *op. cit.*, and R. S. Peters, *Authority, Responsibility, and Education* (London: Allen and Unwin, 1962), ch. 7, "Must an Educator Have an Aim?". [See above, ch. 6. Editor's note.] For earlier attempts to deal with this problem, see Dwayne Huebner, "Moral Perspectives and the Curriculum" in Millard Clements and James B. Macdonald (Eds.), *Moral Dilemmas of Public Schools* (Columbus, Ohio: Charles E. Merrill Books, in press). See also Dwayne Huebner, "Curricular Language and Classroom Meaning," paper delivered at the Research Institute of the Association for Supervision and Curriculum Improvement, Miami, 1965 and to be published in James B. Macdonald (Ed.), *Language and Meaning* (Washington: The Association, in press).

riculum inquiry could fill with meaning. Next, the curriculum specialist needs a conception of value. Ends or objectives are obviously one
form of value, technical in nature, but essential and legitimate in human affairs. However, technical valuing—that is, designating end states
—is not the only form of valuing which must be brought to bear on
educational activity. Once the notion of learning is relegated to a more
appropriate place in curricular thought, then other forms of value
assume a more important role. If determining and realizing value is
an essential aspect of curricular thought, then its counterpart must
also be accepted. Value tends to remain hidden and obscure unless
the activity of criticism is also engaged in. Valuing and criticizing are
two sides of the same coin, and both are essential activities within
curricular endeavors. Finally, with ways to think about educational
activity and its durational nature, and systems of valuing, then the
curriculum specialist becomes a designer of an educative environment.
Through his actions, his fabricating, he constructs an environment
within which the student may live in educationally valuable ways.
These seem to be some of the conceptual problems facing the student
of the curriculum field today. The remainder of this paper will be concerned with some tentative directions for dealing with these problems.

In psychology, man's temporal nature is reflected in the concept of
motivation and learning. The question asked is what pushes man
ahead. The question assumes, it seems to me, a pre-twentieth century
view of man in which stability was the reality and change the problem.
Today change is the reality and stability is the problem. Assuming
that man's life is given by his existence in time and change, the question which should be asked is what holds man back from realizing his
man-nature, his continual capacity for personal evolution and change.
The focus of search is not, then, what makes man grow and learn, or
evolve; but rather what keeps him from so doing, what are the barriers
in his way? Earlier, necessity was the prod, or, as folklore phrases it,
"Necessity is the mother of invention." Today necessity is being taken
care of by technique, which is self-augmenting. So necessity now serves
the cause of technique, and in fact, technique establishes new neces-
sities for men.[14] Necessity no longer gives man the nudge down his
temporal path. I suggest that there are three factors which serve man's
transcendence. The first two, which are interrelated, are language and
social encounter. The third is man's capacity for wonder and awe.

---

[14] See Hannah Arendt, *op. cit.*, chs. 2 and 4.

Heidegger states that language is the ' "house of being" in which man lives.'[15] Through language man participates in the conditioned and the unconditioned. On the one hand, language ties him to the world of necessity and technique by giving him categories for getting around in this world. Language is the key to the puzzling world constructed by his fellow man. Without it, he cannot be a part of this world. On the other hand, language is the instrument of his freedom, the gift which can untie him, temporarily, from his world. It enables him to dream and to see possibilities not yet realized in his life or in his world. It enables him to be aware of values that might be manifest at a later time. Without language he cannot be apart from this world. Because language grows and emerges, men can grow and emerge. The two major vehicles of transcendence found in language are science and poetry.[16] In both, man reaches beyond himself through language. Through both, he contributes to the evolving of others by making new language patterns available. By means of both, he can become aware of what is yet hidden in his world of possibility. Both science and poetry are imaginative disciplines, in which the imagination is tested by appropriate forms of criticism. The dreams of science are criticized by empirical tests and by determining their congruity with other scientific statements. The dreams of poetry are tested by forms of aesthetic criticism, through which value is acknowledged and congruity with other aesthetic forms is determined. The critical act, whether the empirical test or the critical analysis, is the counterthrust which serves to support and to point out weaknesses, and to push the language creator into new realms of being. Hopefully, the imaginative scientist or poet has built into his own working ways some of the appropriate critical methods, but if not, the larger social order provides the necessary criticism. To be introduced into the discipline of science or poetry is to be placed in one of man's temporal pathways, which has boundaries but no fixed ends. The scientist seeks to disprove his theories and to find new ways to express the characteristics of the world as he meets it. To be content with existing theories or existing

---

[15] James M. Robinson and John B. Cobb, Jr. (Eds.), *The Later Heidegger and Theology*, Vol. I: New Frontiers in Theology (New York: Harper and Row, 1963), p. 45.

[16] See John Macmurray, *Reason and Emotion* (New York: Barnes and Noble, 1962); Martin Heidegger, "Holderlin and the Essence of Poetry," in Heidegger, *Existence and Being* (Chicago: Henry Regnery, 1949); R. C. H. Siu, *The Tao of Science* (New York: John Wiley and Sons and the Technology Press, Massachusetts Institute of Technology, 1957); Walker Gibson (Ed.), *The Limits of Language* (New York: Hill and Wang, 1962); James B. Conant, *On Understanding Science* (New Haven, Conn.: Yale University Press, 1947).

ways of explaining the phenomena of the world is to give up the concern for scientific language. Likewise, the poet is never content with prior expressions of his awareness and values. He, too, seeks new language forms which enliven his participation in the world. To use dead language expressions is to be overcome by the inertia of the world as known; but to seek to keep language vital and alive is to contribute to the creation of the world. The joy and the power of language is not that it enables man to fit into the world, but that it leads man beyond the world as presently operating and into a tomorrow which may be better, more beautiful, and more in harmony with the human spirit.

Man's confrontation with man is also a vehicle of transcendence[17]— through conversation, argument, love, economic conflict, and cooperation, even war and hate, and simply by comparison. To be face to face with a man who speaks differently, wants other things, has other ways of life, or who sees the world differently is to be confronted with the inherent questions: "Who am I?" "Who is he?" and "Why are we the way we are?" If the questions are not dealt with honestly and openly, then they are eventually forced upon the confronters by conflict of interest, as is happening today in the integration battles, and the political and economic conflicts in our world. Inherent in each human confrontation is the possibility of growth and transcendence, for as man meets man, he meets the other: someone who differs and consequently someone who manifests other qualities of life and human value. The thinking, feeling, and seeing of others points to the way that I think, feel, and see, and suggests that the world that I think is out there is not the same world that the other thinks is out there. The inherent tension which exists between people because they do differ is, or can be, the source of new life and possibility. The question that must be asked is not "How can man learn to make social encounters vehicles of human transcendence?" but "What are the barriers in today's conditioned world, in the world of technique and necessity, which prevent man's realization of his temporal nature?"

Finally, man's capacity for wonder and awe is a potential vehicle for transcendence or temporal movement. Awe and wonder point to a world beyond man's ken, a world which invites his involvement at ever new levels of existence. Science, art, and religion can all be instrumentalities to this awe and wonder, but the confrontation of men with the

---

[17] Martin Buber, *I and Thou*, translated by Ronald Gregor Smith (New York: Charles Scribner's Sons, 1937).

non-man made is its source. Man-made things and man-made customs constantly put before us conditioned man and his trappings. To have man-made things and conventions stripped away by a new scientific discovery, a new technological invention, or a new art work, thus suddenly uncovering or discovering that which was there all the time, is awe producing. The moment of awe is the moment of humility, when one becomes aware of what one is and is not. To paraphrase Abraham J. Heschel, wonder is the beginning of awe, awe is the beginning of wisdom.[18]

The significance of science is not simply that we understand the world and the tools for its use, but that the world becomes a response-world, as witness the notion of anti-matter or the DNA molecule. The significance of art is not that beauty is produced, but that our eyes are opened to see differently. The significance of technique is not that necessity is cared for, but that our senses are extended—witness the awesome microscopic world and the world under the sea. To have frequent confrontations between man and the awe-producing world of not-man is to again start one on the road of his temporality and change. For through this moment of awe or wonder, the individual can realize how inadequate his existing ways of behavior and thinking are; he recognizes how much of the world escapes his grasp, and how much there is yet to be known or valued or experienced. Why is it, then, that the confrontation between man and not-man does not always result in transcendence and growth? Probably not because man has not learned to respond, but because the world of awe and wonder has been hidden by necessity, technique, and truthless language. Perhaps it is better to remain speechless, awed, with a child who is overcome by a sunset than to say "How beautiful," thus labeling and reducing to trite words an experience which transcends words and men.

Man's temporal quality, his life in time, is partially assured if language, human encounter, and the encounter with the awesome world of the non-man made are seen, not as aspects of necessity, but as the life-giving sources of man's spirit. Man's participation in this ambiguous world of necessity and freedom, or of the conditioned and the unconditioned, is characterized by his use of language, his meetings with others, and his encounters with the non-man-made world. Language is a token of man's necessity, a key element in his technique. But it is

---

[18] Abraham J. Heschel, *God in Search of Man: A Philosophy of Judaism* (New York: Farrar, Strauss, 1955).

also his major vehicle of freedom of his spirit, his most powerful way of escaping the clutches of technique. The social encounter with others is necessary in this complex social and economic world, and social ways are conditioned. But social encounters can be pathways to a future which can emerge. The meeting of man with not-man may be seen as man using the world or gaining mastery over it by technique. But it is also a source of joy and freedom, an invitation to growth and evolution if man can stay open and receptive to it. These, then, are some ways of talking about human movement through time. The possible emergence of man can be seen as he uses language, meets others, and confronts the world. The emergent or transcending participation in language, social encounter, or the non-man-made world could be dimensions of educational activity.

The problem of value is a tricky ethical and axiological one. I cannot hope to deal with it, nor am I capable of doing so. It seems to me that one of its most personal manifestations is the question that we all ask, "Who am I and what is the meaning of my life?" The larger question that the philosopher or artist or religious leader asks is, "Who is Man?" These are questions that have no final answers. The nature of man with a capital M and the nature of each individual man continues to be disclosed to man as the world evolves. It is hinted as the artist creates new works, as the spiritual leader receives new insights, as the philosopher shapes new awareness, as the scientist discovers new principles, and as man conflicts and communes with other men and the natural world. Because it is a difficult problem, the search for value continues, controversy rages, and individuals flounder and seek solace in a variety of rituals or answers. Curriculum specialists seek to sidestep the difficulty of clear statements of goals. Critics continue to hammer away at these goals. This is not because either are right or wrong, but because the emergence and formulation of value requires dialogue and struggle as the world emerges. Our hurt feelings should be turned into joy because we are getting help in identifying and realizing new values in and for educational activity. But we clearly should stop trying to resolve the difficulty by finding the purpose of education or by providing teachers with simplified philosophies of education which discourage them from asking, "Who am I and why am I living like this in my classroom?" or which dissuade them from exploring the similarities and differences between the concept of man discussed in education courses and the concept of man basic to their religious beliefs. Education, if it is looked upon not simply as a profession or as a way of making a living but as a vocation in the sense of a calling, or even as an honest attempt to live fully, is one of the finest life styles for discovering again and again the nature of existence as lived—for the unearthing of value.

Clearly, one form of value is an instrumental form in terms of what it accomplishes or where it leads. But life lived has value not only because it produces something or ends somewhere. This is to turn present life into a commodity for a future state it offers. Life does have value because it gets one to tomorrow or next year. But there may be no tomorrow, and then, of course, life today would have been of no value. Life as lived, in the present moment, has its own values—you know, the "lilies of the field" and "the birds of the air."

The characteristics of educational activity described above, language, human encounter, and awe or wonder would seem to be manifestations of what might be called moral value; that is, one of the ways of valuing activity in the present moment is by asking whether the activity reflects man and his possibilities. Is this moment as we are living it the best that man is capable of? Does it reflect what I believe to be the nature of man and his encounters with the world? Does it help the student perceive the transcending possibilities in language and human encounter, the possibility of wonder and awe in the world of nature and art? Of course there are different moral value systems or views of what man is or can be, hence again the need for discourse and argument and political action. But to attract attention away from the present moment by asking only "What is being learned?" or "What are the expected outcomes?" is to remove educational activity from the moral into only the technical sphere. The valuing process, conceived in terms of means-ends evaluation, forces education into the realm of man's technique, or perhaps technique's man, and away from the realm of man's spirit as a temporal being.

Criticism of the schools and of education, which is the counterthrust necessary for the evolution of educational value, requires attention to moral values manifest in educational activity.[19] This form of criticism is not simply carping, but is penetrating evaluation by educated and disciplined people, aware of the moral dimensions of man's life in today's world. Schools of education have been deficient in that they have not trained teachers to be social or moral critics of educational activity.

---

[19] As one form of such criticism see Harvey Cox, *The Secular City* (New York: The Macmillan Company, 1965).

Beside the sphere of moral values may be placed the sphere of aesthetic values. All more or less permanent artifacts, routines or rituals, and organizational structures may be detached from the world of use and hence be interpreted as symbols with aesthetic dimensions. Likewise all completed chunks of human activity, even though unique, may be looked back upon as having form and unity, and consequently as having aesthetic dimensions. Therefore the components of the educational environment and indeed educational activity itself may be valued aesthetically. Two dimensions of aesthetic value are directly applicable to the educational environment and activity. First, because of its distancing from use, its ability to stand outside of the realm of technique, the object or structure or patterned activity has a form. Thus it has a sense of wholeness, of design, of harmony and balance. It may be said to have the potential for beauty. Likewise, separated from use, the object, structure, or activity becomes symbolic of the artist-creator and indeed of man and society. Symbolically it has the potential for truth in that it symbolizes the feelings, awareness, visions, and possibilities of the artist and his world. Educational activity and the environment in which it occurs may be valued for its beauty and truth. Does it reflect good design, is it harmonious, balanced? Does it symbolize what the teacher really is, and what man is or what man can be? The teacher at the end of an activity or day can ask, "Was this a beautiful day for me and for the students—balanced, harmonious, tension producing and reducing?" "Was it a day filled with truth, that is, did it symbolize what life really is and can be like?" This is an extremely significant form of valuing, and aesthetic criticism could be a powerful way of exposing what education and teaching means to teachers and administrators. Look at educational buildings or architectural structures—do they reflect man's spirit or his technique, man's freedom or his necessity? Search for beauty and truth in the materials used in classroom—they are not there. Instead will be found evidence of education's commitment to technique and the world of consumption. Observe a teacher's behavior and classroom procedures for design and harmony, for the dramatic qualities that heighten life. Infrequently is beauty found; more often, there is simply the ugliness of dead routine. Observe that same behavior as symbolic of that teacher's feelings and meanings of life. Some teaching, effective from a means-ends valuing system, is symbolic of feelings and means which should not exist in schools. Valued aesthetically, educational activity and environment take on new perspectives. Aesthetic criticism is a form of evaluation infrequently brought to bear on education. It is also a disciplined activity, requiring an educated eye, a sense of design, and an awareness of modern man. Schools of education do little to encourage aesthetic forms of valuing and criticism.

The central, most significant, part of curriculum, however, is not value but educational activity itself. Activity takes place within an environment. The designing and fabrication of this environment is the task of the curriculum specialist. Indeed, it might be appropriate to refer to him as a curriculum designer. Discussions of value have consequences in the educational environments that result. To ask, "What is the purpose of education?" is to ask about the characteristics of the school as a place to live.[20] But to ask, "What moral and aesthetic values should be manifest in educational activity?" is also to ask about the characteristics of the school as a place to live.

To build an environment which structures educational activity means to select content from the whole, wide, wonderful world and to make it available for students. So conceived, content is that which is available in the classroom for educational activity. This includes man-made objects, aspects of the natural world grouped or organized in certain ways, symbol or language systems, and usages or social conventions. In fact, educational content becomes a selection of man's culture, thus creating a limited culture for the student. But to keep the image clear, it is necessary to use culture the way Tillich uses it. He reminds those who have been over-conditioned by the behavioral scientist that the biologist uses it differently: "Culture, cultura, is that which takes care of something, keeps it alive, and makes it grow."[21] The curriculum designer fabricates an educational environment which takes care of students, keeps them alive, and makes them grow. The teacher, to use technical language, has an ambiguous role. On the one hand, he represents one part of the content, a part of the culture. As a conditioned being, the teacher brings certain language patterns and behavioral usages into the classroom. Thus he is part of the technique and is a technician. But as a representative of man's spirit, of man's freedom, he must also be a free agent in order to realize moral and aesthetic values in educational activity. It is in the teacher and in the teacher's education and continuing education that the major strug-

---

[20] R. S. Peters, *Authority, Responsibility, and Education* (London: Allen and Unwin, 1962).

[21] Paul Tillich, *Systematic Theology*, Vol. III (Chicago: The University of Chicago Press, 1963).

gle between man's techniques and man's spirit is waged. This is what makes teaching such a significant life activity today, for the teacher epitomizes more sharply than anyone else this twentieth century struggle, engaged as he is in the confrontation of youth becoming aware of a destiny and a social group trying to determine what that destiny will be. The size of institutionalized education makes the struggle even more significant, for educational organizations, administrative structures and styles, and educational materials—all technical devices to achieve ends efficiently—help shape the course of the teacher's struggle.

The design of educational environment and activity requires technical skill. It is in the design and fabrication of the environment that the means-end qualities of traditional curricular thought bear fruit. The most exciting evidence of this is seen in the vigor with which the new media specialists have taken up the cry, "Define your objective behaviorally!" and have adopted the label, "learning technology," as they begin to build instruments and systems for instruction.[22] In the construction of new materials and devices, learning theory has its maximum application in education. The use of theories of learning and behavior for the construction of materials is like the use of physical theories in the design of new buildings, roadways, instruments of communications, and weapons. They change the characteristics of the environment in which we live, and bring forth new responses from those who live in that environment.

Technology in the schools makes three significant contributions to the educational environment. The first is the externalization of a language system into tangible form. Textbooks and information books are tangible, and they serve to put the student into the same language community with scientists or scholars or workers. New developments in programming increase the opportunity to externalize dialogue, and thus increase the possibility of starting the student on one of the paths of language transcendence, for example, language laboratories. Next, technology increases the opportunity for personal encounters via telephone hookups, television, tapes, letters, and finally by way of the arts, wherein the student has distinct opportunities for the "Who am I?" comparison, as he is projected into the lives and feelings of others. Third, as extensions of man's senses[23] technology makes possible new confrontations of the student with the non-technical and increases the opportunity for the experience of awe and wonder. Again art and

---

[22] Robert Glaser, op. cit.
[23] Marshall McLuhan, op. cit.

poetry are examples, the microprojector is another, as can be television and film. The media specialists lose some of their power when they seek to install all media into existing techniques of education. As Mc-Luhan has said, the medium is the message, opening up new vistas of man and his possibilities. The media specialist could also ask, "What does this new technology suggest about man and his possibilities?" and "What kind of educational value can it have in schools?" not simply "How can it facilitate learning?" As Mumford pointed out, the neo-technique is to serve man, not to be served by man.[24] Hence technical developments for education must seek to realize moral and aesthetic values in educational activity as well as technical values. Only in this way can concern for man remain uppermost.

Of course, the educational environment, and consequently educational activity, is limited by time, space, and money. So choices must be made among values to be manifested and content to be included in the classroom. Some values and content are rather universally accepted. For instance, all agree that one educative activity is reading. Some argument about reading is technical argument; for example, which method is most economical? Hopefully, from now to the end of time more efficient methods will evolve that will give teachers greater choice as they teach reading. The search for *the* way to design reading activity is absurd. The search for the most economic way is not, but economics is a subvalue within technique. The argument over text or trade book is perhaps really an argument about the book content of the educational environment. But other aspects of educational content do not find universal agreement. Here, then, the public discussions about aims or ends is part of a vast ideological[25] struggle over control of educational content. This ideological struggle is a reflection of the changing social scene, in terms of new conditions of social life, but also in terms of new social groups gaining ascendency in the power hierarchy. The ideological struggle is necessary as a form of value clarification as the society evolves and meets new problems and possibilities. It is necessary for the evolution of new educational forms and structures. No person, not even the professional educator, can be omniscient about the future characteristics of the society and the consequent shape of educational environments and activities. Consequently the educator needs to accept and participate in constructive social criticism about educational content and to engage in the po-

---

[24] Lewis Mumford, *op. cit.*

[25] See Karl Mannheim, *Ideology and Utopia* (New York: Harcourt, Brace and Company, 1936).

litical process which is man's way of building his social environment.

What is the role of the curricular specialist in this political process? As the fabricator and designer of educational environments, he seeks in the school a just environment for all members of the society. Tillich states that "justice is the uniting function in the individual man and in the social group."[26] The curriculum maker must strive to create an educative environment which represents the values and valued content of all involved social groups, including, as one involved group, the students. The content of the school has shifted as the political process has indicated that now one group, now another, needed attention or gained control. When no one else speaks for an important or neglected group or set of values, then the educator must. He must represent none, yet all. To the extent that he takes unjustified sides, he ruins his effectiveness as the educational adjudicator. As dispassionately as the judge in the law court, he must listen to all sides, including the prophets, and seek to build a just educative environment. Today the curriculum maker is being helped by others who finally care enough about the schools to help in the construction of a just and moral educational environment. The curriculum designer is thus freed from the overburdening responsibility of doing all, and gradually he can begin to see the forest as well as the trees. This is an opportunity for which he has perhaps been waiting and which he should by all means use. The study of curriculum is really the heart and soul of the study of education. All of man's knowledge, wisdom, and skill is required to build a just educational environment. The study of curriculum can be and should be a great liberal and liberating study, for through it the specialist must come to grips with the great social and intellectual problems of today. The study of curriculum need not be the search for curriculum theory, although eventually a theory or theories may emerge. The study of curriculum need not be labeled as a profession, for prestige follows from work, not labels. Is it possible, now that we are partially freed from the vision-hindering busy work, that we can begin to make efforts to grasp the overall design of curriculum and to see how man's evolving techniques can be made subservient to man's evolving spirit? Educational environment and activity in the schools are symbolic of what man is today and what he wants to be tomorrow. The design of these symbols is a great art. The study of curriculum should be a preparation for this artistry.

---

[26] Paul Tillich, *Love, Power, and Justice* (New York: Oxford University Press, 1954), p. 55.

C. J. B. Macmillan and James E. McClellan
Temple University

VIII. CAN AND SHOULD MEANS-ENDS REASONING BE USED IN TEACHING?

INTRODUCTION: ANALYTICAL TABLE OF CONTENTS

I. NOT ALL ANSWERS TO "WHY DID HE DO IT?" USE THE MEANS-ENDS PATTERN OF REASONING

Consider an example. Rabbit is dancing the Texas Star; the movements are prescribed by the caller and the tradition of the dance. At one point in the set, Rabbit takes the hand of Emily, the prettiest of the girls. Observing this, a spectator might wonder about the movement, while not doubting that the action is correctly described as "taking Emily's hand," i.e., that it is to be viewed as an intentional act, done knowingly, and that none of the challenges which would show it to be non- or unintentional holds.[1] We consider this example, because it will enable us to explicate more clearly the means-ends pattern of reasoning than would direct attention to teaching. This example and the others that follow show deliberate actions on the part of an agent— actions that are explained and justified by means-ends reasoning. We assume that teaching also involves deliberate action, although there may be uses of 'teach' which are not essentially connected with intentional action;[2] attention to simple but analogous cases will enable us to illustrate the means-ends pattern without getting confused in issues that are peculiar to teaching.

There are at least three ways of answering the question "Why did Rabbit take Emily's hand?". These are not mutually exclusive: a person might give all three answers or two of them. (Mixed motives are possible.) Although only one uses the means-ends pattern, all contain references to Rabbit's purpose:

1. He took her hand in order to obey the rules of the dance, which required precisely that movement.
2. He took her hand in order to express his affection for her.
3. He took her hand in order to make her father angry.[3]

---

[1] Here are some of the challenges: "I didn't know I was doing *that*." "Somebody pushed me." "I was forced to do it."

G. E. M. Anscombe discusses these challenges at some length in *Intention* (Ithaca, N.Y.: Cornell University Press, 1957), 2nd ed., 1963. See also Charles Taylor, *The Explanation of Behavior* (New York: The Humanities Press, 1964), pp. 54-71.

These are complicated issues. They are raised herein where specifically revelant to claims about means and ends and not to intentional acts in general. See below, Sections II and III.

[2] Such as the answer to "Who taught you that?" when no one engaged in actions intended to produce the learning: "The stove taught me not to touch hot burners." Cases like this are parasitic upon the full-blown case of a teacher engaging in teaching actions.

[3] Idiomatically, one could signal the differences here by use of phrases different from 'in order to': (a) He took her hand *because* one of the rules of the dance required that movement. (b) He took her hand *as* an expression of his affection for her. We use 'in order to' to emphasize that the distinctions we're pursuing are logical, not syntactical.

Only the third of these involves the means-ends pattern. Yet each is a way of describing and explaining or justifying the action of taking Emily's hand. A few words about the first two are necessary for they must be distinguished from the pattern in any claim that it is not the exclusive way of describing, explaining, or justifying rational action.

The first answer explains Rabbit's act by putting it in the context of a wider rule-directed activity: the act is required if one is engaged in the dance, which is *constituted* by a set of such rule-directed movements, and a person not following the rule could be described either as not dancing or as dancing incorrectly. It is worthy of note that under this description one cannot distinguish the action's result from the action itself. Doing the act *is* producing the result; they are not separately describable. We shall call this the "constitutive" pattern of reasoning, for the rules constitute or define the wider activity.

The second answer explains Rabbit's act by more completely describing it as a way of performing another action. It is not that taking Emily's hand is a means to the further goal of showing affection; rather, taking her hand *is* showing affection as governed by a social convention. It is not *by* taking her hand but rather *in* taking her hand that Rabbit shows his affection. Although he may have some further purpose for showing affection, the description "showing affection" does not state it. But it would be wrong to treat this as if it were merely the constitutive way of describing and explaining the action, only with a different set of rules, for he could have expressed affection in some other way—whispered softly, winked, etc.—whereas he could not have performed the same dance except by taking her hand.

There are various ways of taking Emily's hand, of course, but if the move is prescribed as "take the hand of your opposite's partner," then there is no way of doing the dance properly and not taking her hand. There might be other descriptions of taking her hand which appeal to more minute aspects of the movement, but making the move itself is not something that one can avoid and still perform the dance. If taking her hand is showing her his affection, then it is a way of showing affection, and showing affection is a way of taking her hand. We call this the "interpretive pattern" for in using it one interprets the action by reference to its purpose. To give this description is not necessarily to say that Emily understood his action this way; something could have prevented it. It is parallel to Rabbit's saying "I love you," to a deaf girl, which is properly described as "saying 'I love you' " even though she doesn't hear it.[4]

The third answer, of course, uses the means-ends pattern of reasoning. Here Rabbit is described as trying to achieve some result beyond the action, a result that is separately describable and contingently related to the action. This differs importantly from the first two ways of describing, explaining, or justifying the action. We should note certain obvious features of Emily's angry father: his anger is clearly different from Rabbit's hand taking; the two events are contingently related; the anger may very well be the results of Rabbit's action. But from the following two facts: (a) Rabbit then took Emily's hand in order to make Emily's father angry, and (b) at the same time Emily's father got angry, it does not follow that her father got angry *because* of Rabbit's action. When actions and results are thus contingently related, the occasion is set for the means-ends pattern of reasoning. The next section is devoted to explicating this pattern in a somewhat more formal fashion.

II. SIX PRINCIPLES DEFINE
THE MEANS-ENDS PATTERN OF REASONING

Imagine a man wielding an axe; he is being fairly systematic and skilled in his use of the instrument; the object of his axeological affections is a tall pine tree. Two passersby stop to watch. One asks, "What is he doing?" The second replies, "He's chopping."

One: "Why?"

Two: "To bring the tree down." or "To fell it."

Here is a relatively clear case of the pattern used to describe and explain an activity: a simple description of an *activity* as "chopping," and an explanation of the chopping by reference to the *expected result*, bringing down the tree. The dialogue might have gone differently and still have stayed within the bounds of the means-ends pattern. The question "What is he doing?" might have been answered by "Chopping the tree down." The goal or purpose or expected result of

---

[4] These two patterns differ as necessary and sufficient conditions: In the constitutive pattern, taking her hand is a necessary (but not sufficient) condition of doing the dance; while in the interpretive pattern, taking her hand is a sufficient (but not necessary) condition of showing affection. Both, of course, explain the action by relating it to otherwise describable actions.

the action here serves as a description as well as an explanation of the activity.

But even actions described by specification of their objectives do not *require* means-ends explanations or justifications. Of the description "He is felling the tree" for example, one may ask "Why?" and receive answers of either means-ends or non-means-ends types:

a) "In order to make firewood."
b) "In order to do his job." (Which might be either a constitutive or an interpretive explanation; we cannot decide which.)

Either a or b might be the appropriate explanation of the action, and there are ways of telling which is the correct one in specific cases. For example:

a) he does not take care to prevent breakage of the tree; he proceeds (later) to do certain other things, etc.;
b) he follows certain job rules, works with others, etc.

This illustrates our first general point: *the question whether the means-ends pattern applies is a question of fact and not of concept.*

Let us note the logical relationships between "He is chopping the tree" (P) and "He is felling the tree" (Q):

i) The truth of P and Q vary independently of one another: both P and Q may be true; P may be true, Q false (the most determined attack on a sequoia with a boy scout hatchet is unlikely to fell it); P may be false, Q true (perhaps he is using a bulldozer); both P and Q may be false.

ii) Under appropriate circumstance, i.e., when his point in chopping is to fell the tree, Q serves as an explanation or justification of P (which is not to say that it is necessarily a good explanation or a full justification).

iii) But even where P and Q are both true, Q is not necessarily the explanation or justification of P; even though he is chopping and the action is resulting in the tree's being felled, he may be chopping in order to do something quite different: kill a vine, exercise, produce a chip of a certain size, etc.

Since these logical relations are so complex, how does one tell whether a person is using the means-ends pattern of reasoning? We propose to answer this question first by examining the ways in which the use of the pattern could be wrong, in order to see what must be the case for its use to be correct. Keep in mind the woodchopper and passersby mentioned above; we will modify the example as we go along.

There are at least six ways in which one might challenge the use of the means-ends pattern in describing, explaining or justifying an action.

1. The original description could be incorrect: in saying "He's chopping," one might have been mistaken, as for instance, if he had seen only the backswing and what the agent was doing then was removing the axe from a cut which had been made earlier; the correct description would not be "chopping," but something else. The pattern might be used, but under a different description, e.g., "Why is he removing the axe?". Here "Why is he chopping?" is challenged as a relevant question by "He's not chopping at all."

2. The activity could have no objective. If a person cannot state or otherwise show what objective he is trying to reach by his action, then *that person* cannot use the pattern to describe, explain, or justify the action. As answers to the question "What is your objective in chopping?", "I don't know" or "I have none" deny the applicability of the pattern. Thus, a woodchopper who cannot tell us what he is trying to achieve by the chopping (e.g., the tree's falling, the vine's being severed, getting his wage) cannot make his action clear by using the means-ends pattern. Perhaps *he* cannot make it clear at all, although perhaps someone else could. The shift from the passerby to the woodsman himself does not affect the logic of the argument; no person can explain or justify an action—his own or another's—by using the pattern if he cannot state or show the objective.

3. The achievement of the objective might be a logically necessary condition for the completion of the action. Suppose the woodsman himself responds to the question "Why are you felling the tree?" by saying "Just to have it fall." There are two different events—his felling the tree and the tree's falling—but it is logically impossible for him to fell the tree without its falling. Given this logical connection, we say the two are "not separately describable."

4. The particular use of the pattern could be refused by the agent. This challenge can be made in two ways: (a) The *agent* could deny the description of his action as taking means to ends. "I'm not chopping" or "I'm practicing my baseball swing" does not defeat "He's chopping" or even "He's felling the tree," but if true, it does defeat any explanation beginning "He's chopping in order to . . . ." Notice how this differs from the first challenge that denies the correctness of "chopping" (as a description of his action) asserted by anyone. (b) If the woodchopper truthfully denies that felling the tree was the result he

intended to achieve by chopping, it follows that the proposed explanation using the means-ends pattern is incorrect. For example, he may convince us that his chopping was done in order to secure a certain size chip for use in a new sculpture. Even though his tree fell, its falling was not the result which explains or justifies his chopping. But this is not to say that no use of the pattern is applicable. Where someone rejects an explanation of his action as leading to a particular result, we may reasonably expect him to explain or justify it in some other way.

5. The connection between the action and the objective could be unintelligible. A person who uses the pattern to explain action implies that there are grounds for believing that it will achieve the objective he claims for it. Thus a man who claims that he is chopping a tree in order to kill his wife must be prepared to show the connection between the two events. The certainty of the knowledge will differ from case to case, being based sometimes on hunches, sometimes on highly sophisticated scientific theories. Whichever is the case, the person using the pattern must be prepared to offer *some* reason for believing that the action will achieve or contribute to the objective.

6. The achievement of the objective could fail to terminate the action: (a) There is something decidedly odd about the man who *says* that he is chopping the tree in order to fell it, but continues chopping when the tree is downed, even though there might be other reasons for continuing and even though these other reasons fit other uses of the means-ends pattern, such as making firewood out of the trunk. Note that the oddness is in the explanation, and not in the action. (b) It is a reasonable challenge to a person's claim that he is chopping in order to fell the tree if the tree's falling does not provide him a reason for stopping chopping.

Our claim is that any use of the means-ends pattern of reasoning is open to any of these challenges and that its user must admit the relevance (if not the correctness) of all of them. If he cannot answer the appropriate question—or if he denies that there are possible answers to them—then we cannot understand what he intends by saying that a given action is a means to a given end. When any of these challenges can be sustained, the use of the pattern fails for logical reasons; it involves the speaker in at best anomolies, at worst self-contradictions.

Now the more difficult task is to move from negative examples to positive principles by which to identify and evaluate the use of the means-ends pattern of reasoning in the description, explanation and justification of action.

Principle 1: The action must be correctly described.

(Violation: "He's chopping in order to fell the tree, but he's not chopping.")

Principle 2: The action must have a describable objective.

(Violation: "There's no purpose for my felling the tree" or "I can't say what the purpose is, and neither can anyone else.")

Principle 3: The objective and the action must be separately describable.

(Violation: "He's [I'm] felling the tree just to have it fall down.")

Principle 4: (a) The description of the action must be accepted by the agent.

(Violation: "Who's chopping? I'm rehearsing for *The Wizard of Oz.*")

(b) The description of the action as done for that result must be accepted by the agent.

(Violation: "I didn't chop in order to fell the tree, but rather to create a situation in which I could demonstrate my honesty, Father dear.")

Principle 5: There must be some grounds for holding that the action will achieve the objective.

(Violation: "There is no reason to believe that chopping this tree will kill my wife, but that's what I'm doing it for.")

Principle 6: There must be some intelligible connection between the achievement of the objective and the termination of the actions done in order to achieve it.

(Violation: "What do you mean, you're chopping in order to fell the tree? It's already down!")

Each of the above principles can be explicated within the following formal schema: Using the means-ends pattern (P) implies that a *certain* relation (R) holds between a certain act (A) and the consequences (B) of that act. In short,

$$P \supset R_{(A, B)}$$

Principle 1 says that to deny A is to deny P; Principle 2 says that to deny B is to deny P; and Principles 3, 4, 5, and 6 specify the specific features that R must exhibit if P is true. We had anticipated that some philosopher had investigated these formal properties of a means-ends logic, but our cursory search of the literature failed to reveal it. Lacking reason to believe otherwise, we hold that Principles 1 and 2 are theorems in *any* means-ends logic. A full logic of means and ends lies at the intersection of formal logic, philosophy of science, and ethics, an intersection often unnoticed by philosophers travelling on only one of the routes.[5]

III. MEANS-AND-ENDS DISCOURSE PROVIDES ONLY A FORMAL PATTERN OF REASONING

The use of the means-ends pattern of reasoning according to these principles guarantees neither (1) the moral rectitude nor (2) the scientific rationality of a person's actions.

1. A person who says that he is engaged in an activity in order to produce some objective must be able to give a description of the objective which shows it to be a good; for instance, a man who offered an explanation of his chopping by saying that he did it in order to produce painful blisters on his hands but refused any of the possible value characterizations of this objective is not entirely comprehensible.[6] But it would be wrong to treat this as a logical weakness in the use of the pattern. We understand the action as done in order to produce the objective, even though we do not understand the man who is doing it: we can understand chopping in order to produce painful blisters, but we cannot understand a person who wants to produce painful blisters *simpliciter*.

If the use of the means-ends pattern does not guarantee *any* value

---

[5] Dewey, for example, considers only reasoning of the sort mentioned in our Principle 5: increasing the rationality of the connection between the means and the end. (*Logic: The Theory of Inquiry* [New York: Henry Holt, 1938], pp. 9-10, 460-62.) J. S. Mill turns from questions of "practical reasoning" to the nature of the scientific ground for the reasoning. (*A System of Logic*, 8th ed. [London: Longmans, 1959], Bk. VI, ch. 12.) Ernest Nagel in *The Structure of Science* (New York: 1961), pp. 490-95, is concerned only with the question of whether the connection between means and ends is value-free. The same question exercises Antony Flew in his article "Ends and Means" in *The Encyclopedia of Philosophy* (New York: The Macmillan Co. and The Free Press, 1967), II, 508-11. Michael Scriven, *Primary Philosophy* (New York: McGraw-Hill, 1966), p. 47-49, treats the problem only as an ethical issue, but not as a logical one. None of these writers considers all of these principles; Professor Guttchen presented a thoughtful discussion of the contrast between Dewey and Mill to the Middle Atlantic States Philosophy of Education Society in May, 1967.

[6] There is always a possible value characterization of any consequence; for instance, painful blisters might be valuable in one of the following ways: pain for him is a pleasure, for he's a masochist; a certain poitical party will take over soon and kill everyone with soft hands, and he wants to live; he just *likes* painful blisters, etc.

characterization of the objective, it follows *a fortiori* that it does not guarantee a morally correct judgment.[7]

2. "I know that you are trying to fell the sequoia, but why use the boy scout hatchet when the chain saw is right there?" Here, again, the chopping is explained on the means-ends pattern, but the person using this particular reason escapes our comprehension if he fails to answer. It is easy to construct answers to this efficiency question: "It's a game," "The wood you cut yourself warms you twice," "Arbuckle won't lend me his saw." But if no answer comes forth, our assumption of the agent's rationality is shaken, even though the chopping itself is explained.

IV. BORDERLINE CASES TEST THE PRINCIPLES

The chopping case was chosen, of course, because it most obviously exemplified the employment of means in order to achieve an end. We must now test whether the principles derived from this obvious case do account for and resolve the more difficult cases where one would be tempted, but hesitates, to use the means-ends pattern. For, after all, teaching is not so obviously a means-ends activity as chopping is.

Two sorts of troublesome cases present themselves for consideration: (a) cases involving unknown purposes; i.e., those in which a man does something for a purpose but does not (consciously?) recognize the purpose for which he acts. The problem here, of course, is to acknowledge that such an action does seem explicable by the pattern even though Principle 4 seems to be violated; (b) another sort of case is that in which the connection between the action and its result seem merest fantasy. The problem here is that reasoning of the most fantastic sort can be fitted into the pattern, but if everything that can be fitted in is allowed, the pattern seems to be quite trivial. Thus a-type cases are those in which the principles seem too strong—they would exclude from the pattern cases that the ordinary man would recognize as following means-ends reasoning. But b-type cases pose the other sort of test to the principles—they would admit instances that the ordinary man would not recognize as reasoning at all. Will the principles survive these tests? Let us see.

---

[7] Recall Miss Anscombe's example of the "desirability characterization" of the Nazi's killing Jewish children as his final act. *Op. cit.*, p. 72-73.

a) There are two ways in which an action can be explained as purposeful while the purpose is unknown. The first is exemplified by the anthropologist who says, "I know that these people are doing this dance for some purpose, but I don't know what the purpose is," or the soldier who says, "I know that I'm fighting the Viet Cong for some purpose, but I don't know what that purpose is." The second way is orthodox psychoanalysis, where the explanation of an action is that the agent is trying to achieve a goal of which he is not conscious.

The first examples are not troublesome. They exemplify a belief that the means-ends pattern provides the appropriate explanation of the actions in question but that the explainer is ignorant of one element in the pattern. The statement "There's an objective, but I don't know what it is" can express either faith in the rationality of the agent, or a principle of investigation, specifying the sort of thing that the investigator is going to search for.

Belief in an unknown purpose could be false, of course. It may be that the war is not fought to achieve *any* result beyond the fighting itself. It may be that *no* result is sought by the dancers subject to anthropological investigation. The falsehood, however, lies not in the pattern but in its use in a particular case; the principles are all operative, but incorrectly so.

A similar problem arises in the use of the means-ends pattern to explain the actions of non-language-using animals. If the animal does not recognize any description of himself, it follows *ipso facto* that he cannot recognize the correctness of the pattern as a description. Yet we do describe animals as doing one thing in order to achieve something else: for example, the chimpanzees observed by Baroness Van Lawick-Goodall are described as making and using tools in order to get water out of tree stumps and termites out of termite hills.[8] Such a description meets all of our criteria except those of the recognition and acceptance of the description.

But this is just an exception to our principles, not a counter-example. For these animals can be described by the means-ends pattern only because we are accustomed to full-blown cases of human action where the agent's true counter-description has precedence over our observer's description. If there were no paradigm cases of acting for consciously held purposes, the description of the chimpanzees would

---

[8] Jane Van Lawick-Goodall, "New Discoveries among Africa's Chimpanzees," *National Geographic*, CXXVI (December, 1965), 802-31.

be impossible; the description is of the chimpanzees acting *as* a man making and using tools would act, but with the unfortunate inability to describe their own action caused by their equally unfortunate lack of language. The means-ends pattern can be used in describing their action because they are doing the same thing a man would do, and its truth in specific cases is subject to the same tests as the ordinary pattern where we are—for some reason—unable to ask the agent if this is his purpose. All of the other principles hold in this truncated use of the means-ends pattern.

Another objection to our principles can easily be anticipated. It might be held that even in human beings who are, in some sense, *capable* of describing actions and intentions, it is often the case that a means-ends pattern of reasoning takes place below the threshold of consciousness, such that the agent does not know what he is really doing, much less his real purpose for doing it. If this is true, then obviously our Principle 4 is too restrictive: the means-ends pattern could be operating in reality though by our principles we would not recognize it.

The literature of psychoanalysis, of course, abounds in instances of unconscious means-ends thinking. Indeed the task of the psychoanalyst, in the classical Freudian conception, may be described as revealing to the agent the means-ends pattern of reasoning he (the agent) has actually been following. Take this typical case from Freud's introductory lectures:

> A young man loses a pencil to which he was much attached. A few days before he had had a letter from his brother-in-law which concluded with these words: "I have neither time nor inclination at present to encourage you in your frivolity and idleness." Now the pencil was a present from this brother-in-law. Had it not been for this coincidence we could not of course have maintained that the loss involved an intention to get rid of the gift. One loses objects when one has quarrelled with the giver and no longer wants to be reminded of him.[9]

There are very many and very technical problems in historical interpretation which we must avoid. For example, did Freud himself actually consider "errors" (such as slips of tongues, loss of possessions, etc.) to be literally *caused* as a loose step might cause a fall or *intended*

---

[9] S. Freud, *A General Introduction to Psychoanalysis* (New York: Washington Square Press, 1960), p. 58.

as, in the quotation, we might intend to lose all reminders of obnoxious acquaintances?[10]

Did Freud propose that terms like 'purpose', 'motive', and 'intention' be taken *literally* when prefaced by 'unconscious', or did he propose merely a metaphorical, as-if, extension of such terms so as to reveal unsuspected aspects of human conduct? Antony Flew inclines to the latter view:

> . . . the kernel of Freud's discovery was this: if you are prepared so to extend such notions as 'motive', 'intention', 'purpose', 'wish', and 'desire' that it becomes proper to speak of motives and so forth which are not known to, and the behavior resulting from which is not under the immediate control of, the person who harbors them, then you can interpret (and even guide) far more of human behavior in terms of concepts of this sort than any sophisticated adult had previously realized.[11]

That is certainly *one* plausible interpretation of psychoanalysis, but it is doubtful that it is Freud's. For the terms cited by Flew are distinctly those used in describing and explaining voluntary action, but Freud (at times, though not at all times) wished to deny the existence of voluntary action and affirm an ineluctable causality (cf. quote from Skinner above) in all psychic phenomena. "The truth is that you have an illusion of a psychic freedom within you which you do not wish to give up. I regret to say that on this point I find myself in sharpest disagreement with you."[12]

At other times, Freud seems to regard the causes of mental phenomena as unconscious purposes or intentions, identical in every respect (except, of course, openness to conscious inspection) to conscious purposes or intentions: "What sort of purposes or tendencies [i.e., the unconscious ones] are these which thus interfere with the other [i.e., conscious] intentions, and what is the relation between the two?"[13]

We mention these very ticklish questions in the philosophical analy-

---

[10] Cf. B. F. Skinner, "Critique of Psychoanalytic Concepts and Theories," *Minnesota Studies in the Philosophy of Science*, I (Minneapolis, Minn.: University of Minnesota Press, 1956), p. 77: "Freud's great contribution to Western thought has been described as the application of the principle of cause and effect to human behavior. . . . This was not, however, Freud's own view of the matter."

[11] Antony Flew, "Motives and the Unconscious," *Minnesota Studies in the Philosophy of Science*, I (Minneapolis, Minn.: University of Minnesota Press, 1956), 155.

[12] Freud, *op. cit.*, p. 52.

[13] *Ibid.*, p. 48.

sis of psychoanalysis just to show that they are there and that the analysis which follows does not answer them. Rather, it would seem, the logic of ordinary language, perhaps under the influence of psycho-analytic discourse, admits of means-ends reasoning on the unconscious level, without the theoretical framework psychoanalysis provides. To illustrate: suppose a young teacher, Miss T, publicly berates a student, Suzie, quite severely and we ask Miss T herself and then one of her psychoanalytically-inclined colleagues why she did it. Miss T might reply, "So that Suzie won't be lazy and sassy in the future." This an-swer would seem to satisfy all the principles of means-ends reasoning. (Which, remember, is not to say that it is good reasoning; these prin-ciples constitute sorting, not grading, criteria.) But suppose her col-league, who knows Miss T quite well, should provide this alternative explanation: "Miss T is not conscious of it, but in fact she is still engaged in a bitter conflict against her younger sister, a girl who re-sembles Suzie not only in appearance but also in gaiety and insouci-ance. When Miss T calls Suzie lazy and sassy, she is actually trying to debate those charms employed by her sister to steal their father's affections."

Let us call Miss T's explanation of her actions E_1, her colleague's E_2. It seems clear that both E_1 and E_2 can be placed in the means-ends sequence. But for E_2 there is the difficulty that neither the description of the action—say, "denigrating and ridiculing a person very like her sister"—nor the end sought—say, "scoring points in a sibling struggle" —would be recognized or accepted by Miss T as describing what she was doing or what she was doing it for. Thus our Principle 4 seems to be violated. Faced with a choice between (a) keeping the principles and regarding E_2 as *not* means-ends reasoning or (b) recognizing that E_2 *is* means-end reasoning and therefore the principles need revision, we should find our analysis in grave jeopardy.

The trick, of course, is that E_2 is not, as it stands, an instance of reasoning at all, at least not in the sense that E_1 is reasoning. Note the obvious difference: Concerning E_1, there is no doubt who is reasoning. Even if E_1 had been offered by the colleague ("Why did she berate Suzie so? Why, to make her less lazy and sassy, I suppose."), we would know that it is Miss T's reasoning that is being discussed. Indeed, if E_1 were offered by a colleague and Miss T should deny it ("I should never have thought it would change Suzie's behavior, but I had hoped my scolding would discourage others following her example."), one would hesitate to accept E_1 as *the* explanation of Miss T's actions.

But this is not the case with E_2. Miss T's vigorous denial that her antipathy to Suzie is related to her feelings toward her sister does not shake our confidence in E_2; on the contrary, the vigor of her denial partially confirms the E_2 hypothesis. Then who is doing the reasoning? We hesitate to hypostatize "Miss T's unconscious" or "Miss T's Id" or any other such agent to do the reasoning. Thus we do not have to accept that E_2 is an instance of means-ends reasoning which requires an adjustment of our principles, for if we cannot say whose reasoning it is, we do not have to call it 'reasoning' at all.

Which is not to deny that E_2 may not indeed be a much more revealing, in some sense a truer, explanation than E_1. Many human actions are not guided by reasoning, means-ends or any other variety. But then our principles do not require us to hold that all descriptions–explanations–justifications of actions fit the pattern. Nor is our argument a denial that indeed E_2 *may* be, indeed, Miss T's reasoning. Perhaps in the course of psychoanalysis, or even simple introspection, Miss T might come to recognize just such intentions behind her hostility to Suzie. In which event, obviously, our Principle 4 would be satisfied.

In summary, when an explanation or justification of an action makes reference to unconscious purposes, we have to ask what is meant. If to say that a person acts for ends of which he is unconscious means that these ends are those he would acknowledge and accept if his fears, anxieties, or embarrassments were removed, then our principles are preserved, though we may have to state them in conditionals rather than in simple declaratives. But if to say that a person acts for unconscious ends means to act for ends that are, in principle, not those he would affirm under the most truth-revealing circumstances, then it is apparent that means-ends language is being used metaphorically rather than literally. Such metaphorical extensions of the pattern may be very revealing ways to talk about human behavior (though there is no necessity that they be), but their existence constitutes no decisive argument against Principle 4.

b) Q: "Why are you chopping the tree?"

   K: "In order to kill my wife, who is away visiting her mother."

   Q: "But why do you believe that chopping the tree will lead to that result?"

   K: "Because my last two wives died just after I chopped a tree down."

Here's K's grounds for believing that his act will result in his wife's death are weak. If such uses of knowledge are admitted under the means-ends pattern of reasoning, the pattern itself seems to be trivial. It admits too much.

But this example shows not a weakness in the pattern, but a weakness in its use in a particular case. K explains his action, but the explanation depends on a dubious belief. K may be irrational, but his irrationality lies outside his use of the pattern.

The cure for that triviality here lies not in rejecting the means-ends pattern, but in using the pattern more rigorously, with greater attention to the evidence for believing that the action will lead to the predicted result.

Summary

We have thus far explicated a pattern of reasoning which seems fairly close to the ordinary pattern used when agents act in order to achieve, bring about, or produce states-of-affairs beyond the actions themselves. We have shown that the six principles of this pattern can be used to demonstrate why important borderline cases are on the borderline. The principles, then, show how and why some extraordinary explanations are extraordinary. This is no small advantage.

V. TEACHING CAN BE DESCRIBED BY THE MEANS-END PATTERN

If teaching implies learning, then teaching is not related to learning as means to ends. For the students' learning then would be evidence that teaching has taken place. This would violate Principle 3, that the activity and the goal be separately describable. Part of the *meaning* of "Smith is teaching math to Johnny" would be "Johnny is learning math from Smith," and we could not describe the teaching as teaching without entailing the learning claim.

But teaching claims and learning claims do not imply one another; for since the two statements, Smith is teaching math to Johnny and Johnny is learning math from Smith, can have any combination of truth values and still make sense,[14] they cannot be related either as

---

[14] That is: Smith can be teaching and Johnny learning; Smith can be teaching and Johnny not learning; Johnny can be learning and Smith not teaching; Smith can be not teaching and Johnny not learning.

synonyms or by implication. But it is *possible* that they are related as means and ends, since this multiplicity of logical possibilities is characteristic of the pattern, as we have seen.[15]

One way to make out the means-ends relationship of teaching and learning is by analyzing 'teach' as a "task verb" and 'learn' as a "parallel achievement verb." If this analysis is correct, there is at least room for the means-ends pattern, for in the paradigms of parallel (or "corresponding") task and achievement words, the principles of the pattern are met: one races in order to win; the doctor treats in order to cure. Many philosophers of education have analyzed teaching-learning as task and achievement.[16] Unfortunately, this analysis is unsuccessful, for the task and achievement distinction is not subtle enough to contain teaching and learning. In showing why this is the case, we can bring out the important features of these concepts.

B. O. Smith has argued most clearly that 'teach' is a task verb, of which the "corresponding achievement" is 'learn':

> Task words are those that express activities, such as "racing", "treating", "travelling", and "hunting." The corresponding achievement words are "win", "cure", "arrive", and "find." *Teaching* is a task word and *learn* is the parallel achievement word. Achievement words signify occurrences or episodes. Thus one wins, arrives, or finds a particular moment, or a cure is effected at a particular time. Nevertheless some achievement verbs express a continued process. A boat is launched at a particular instant but it is held at the dock for inspection. On the other hand, task verbs always signify some sort of activity or extended proceedings. We can say of a task such as play, treat, or teach that it is performed skillfully, carefully, successfully, or ineffectively. We may play the game successfully or unsuccessfully, but we cannot win unsuccessfully. We may treat a patient skillfully or unskillfully, but the restoring of health is neither skillful nor unskillful. It makes sense to say that we teach unsuccessfully, but it is self-contradictory to say we learned French unsuccessfully.[17]

---

[15] Sections I and II above.

[16] The source for the distinction is Gilbert Ryle, *The Concept of Mind* (New York: Barnes and Noble, 1949), pp. 149-52. Educational philosophers using it include B. O. Smith, "A Concept of Teaching," in B. O. Smith and Robert H. Ennis (Eds.), *Language and Concepts in Education* (Chicago: Rand McNally, 1961), pp. 88-90; [See above, Ch. II. Editor's Note.] Israel Scheffler uses something like this in his distinction between "success" and "intent" senses of 'teach' in *The Language of Education* (Springfield, Ill.: Charles C Thomas, 1960), pp. 39-40; R. S. Peters uses the task-achievement distinction to analyze 'education' in *Ethics and Education* (Chicago: Scott Foresman, 1967), but claims that 'education' is an "achievement" word. This way of analyzing 'teach' is rather widely accepted without critical attention.

[17] Smith, *op. cit.*, p. 90.

Teaching, on the task-achievement view, is logically parallel to "looking for the thimble," and the students' learning is parallel to "finding the thimble."

Note that the paradigms of corresponding task and achievement verbs (racing–winning, treating–curing, traveling–arriving, hunting–finding) are all verbs that have the same subject, and that 'teaching' and 'learning' in their paradigm uses must have different subjects. This is not a decisive objection, for we may (by appropriate verbal squiggling) translate 'learn' into 'getting . . . to learn'; 'teach' (as task) is parallel to "getting the student to learn" (as achievement). But several other objections *are* decisive.

The nature of this task-achievement relation varies. When "trying to" plus achievement verb can be substituted for the corresponding task verb without change of meaning or truth value, we call the relation strongly parallel, otherwise weakly parallel. Thus "hunting for a wife" and "finding a wife" are strongly parallel, "running a race" and "winning a race" are weakly parallel. For we simply would not know what to make of the assertion that a man was hunting for a wife but not trying to find one (except as a paradoxical or ironic way of saying something very different from either of these). But it is not at all odd for a man to run a race without trying to win the race—perhaps he is out for the exercise or companionship; perhaps he is lazy.

Now the difficulty with treating 'teaching' and 'get to learn' as parallel task-achievement verbs is that the pair of expressions is neither strongly nor weakly parallel. The relation is not weakly parallel, for we could not understand (without a great deal more questioning) a man who claimed that he was teaching somebody something but denied that he was trying to get that something across to that somebody. The parallel is not so weak that 'teach' can be separated from its parallel 'trying to,' as these paradigmatic weak parallels can be.

On the other hand, the relation is not strongly parallel, for getting somebody to learn something is not necessarily what one is doing when one is teaching. There well may be other objectives one is trying to reach. We can well understand a comment like the following: "I'm teaching my class quadratic equations, but I'm not trying to get them to learn quadratic equations but rather to get them to appreciate the abstract quality of mathematical reasoning." Thus in the discussion of the weak parallel, we had to shift from "trying to get someone to learn something" to "trying to get something across to somebody," the latter expression being broad enough to encompass what we may call non-learning objectives (NLO's); those objectives which signal their presence by such locations as 'understand,' 'grasp,' 'comprehend,' 'appreciate,' and (perhaps) others. The proper analysis of NLO's is another task that we cannot undertake here; their existence, however, is sufficient ground for denying that 'teaching' and 'trying to get to learn' are strongly parallel.[18]

One obvious attack on our argument can be easily rebutted. Taking a strongly parallel set of expressions like 'shooting at the bear' and 'hitting the bear,' an opponent to our argument might attack it by posing this example; "I'm shooting at the bear, not just to hit the bear but rather to protect the child whom the bear is about to mangle." But this sentence, understandable in itself, is not a counter-example to our denial of strong parallel. For protecting-the-child is *not* a non-hitting-the-bear objective, but rather a *further* objective for the achievement of which hitting the bear is necessary. We assume, of course, that the speaker is using words fairly precisely when he says he is shooting *at* the bear; he does not mean 'near' or 'toward' or 'in the general vicinity of,' each of which has its own strongly parallel 'hitting' achievement.

There is a final and conclusive reason for not regarding 'teaching' and 'getting to learn' as corresponding task and achievement verbs. To explain, let us first note why any task and achievement verbs are called corresponding; they correspond in that trying to achieve is necessarily doing the task, not in that doing the task is necessarily trying to achieve. But there is not any necessity in the relation between 'teach' and 'learn.' Trying to get someone to learn is not necessarily teaching, for there are restrictions of manner and motive on teaching which do not apply, say to propagandizing, conditioning, hypnosis, or lobotomy—any one of which (under suitable conditions) could be an instance of trying to get someone to learn something.[19]

These same objections to treating 'teach' and 'get to learn' as cor-

---

[18] The class of NLO's *may* be limited to mental acts (like understanding, appreciating, believing, knowing, thinking, wondering, supposing, etc.) which may be induced or "set off" by teaching. The analysis of the relationships between these and teaching would require another volume or two. Suffice it here to say that these are not all to be classed as learning, but that teaching may legitimately aim at one or more of them. "Teaching a poem" is not necessarily trying to get the students to learn the poem. For a beginning on "mental acts" see Peter Geach, *Mental Acts* (New York: Humanities Press, 1957).

[19] For discussions see Scheffler, *op. cit.*, p. 57; and Thomas F. Green, "A Topology of the Teaching Concept." *Studies in Philosophy and Education*, III (Winter, 1964-65), 284-319. [See above, Chs. III and IV. Editor's Note.]

responding task and achievement verbs apply to Israel Scheffler's distinction between "intention" and "success" uses of the term "teach."[20] For Scheffler means by "success," success in inducing learning. And the existence of NLO's counts against that limitation on success equally as it counts against 'getting to learn' as the achievement for which 'teach' is the corresponding task. And it has also been argued that eventually lack of success would count against the claim that teaching, even in the intentional sense, has occurred.[21] No doubt Scheffler would be willing to broaden his criteria of success and to explain in more detail exactly how these two senses of 'teach' are related. Nor do we doubt that B. O. Smith and others can patch up the task-achievement analysis to take account of the objections we have raised. But we have made enough of the matter to be able to draw this conclusion: the task-achievement analysis is a special case of the means-ends pattern; one in which means and ends are more conceptually related than they are in the pattern generally. But this restricted version of the pattern does not fit teaching easily or naturally. We should advise, then, that analytic effort which might go into repairing these damages in the task-achievement analysis be devoted instead to the subtleties actually present when teaching is taken as a means to a whole range of mental acts (and further goals) as ends.

Thus in the general means-ends pattern we can raise and answer the question of what is to count as teaching. Does "trying to teach" signify "teaching" or doing something else, as "trying to hide" is something other than "hiding?" How is it that we may borrow "He's getting them to learn (or understand, or grasp, or . . . .) something" to signify teaching that has a fine chance of success? While "There's no possibility of their learning that theorem" can be used to deny that whatever he is doing will count as teaching?

So how can the pattern be used to decide what will count as teaching? Here is one answer:

The truth of a description of a person as teaching depends on evidence: such descriptions are not "low-level" or primary descriptions to be "read off" from the world, like the names of colors. Asked "Why do you say that Arnold is teaching?", one cannot just say "Look at him: that's *called* teaching," as one can answer "Why do you say the ball is red?" by saying "That's what's *called* red." The answer is given

---

[20] Scheffler, *op. cit.*, esp. pp. 42-46 and 60-75.
[21] Colin Campbell, "A Comment on Whether Teaching Implies Learning." *Harvard Educational Review* (Winter, 1965), pp. 82-83.

by giving "lower-level" descriptions of actions which—in appropriate contexts—*constitute* teaching.

But the problem is, how do we know which acts (what sort of acts) constitute teaching? What are the criteria by which we decide that a given act *counts* as teaching?

In part, the means-ends pattern gives us an answer to this: where the answer to a question "Why are you doing that?" can be answered either by "Because I'm teaching . . ." or "In order that they learn (understand, etc.) . . . ," the act in question *counts as* teaching.

1. "Why are you writing that list of parts of speech on the blackboard?"
   a) "Because I'm teaching them the parts of speech, and I've found that students learn them better when they are summarized on the board."
   b) "In order that they (understand) learn the parts of speech, and I've found . . ."
2. "Why are you telling them the story of George Washington and the cherry tree?"
   a) "I'm teaching them about the character of the founding father of our country."
   b) "In order that they understand the character of the founding father."
3. "Why are you arching your eyebrows like that?
   a) "I'm teaching them to be critical of remarks like those that Vera just made, and this is my way of expressing doubt."
   b) "In order that they learn to be critical of remarks."

In all of these cases, the explanation is given in two ways: first by a teaching claim and second by specifying the end to be achieved by the action. Where such questions can be answered in both of these ways without change of meaning or truth, the act explained counts as teaching. We might say that it *constitutes* teaching in each case.

There are relevant questions to be asked, of course, which might throw doubt on whether the act will achieve its intended results—questions about the evidence for the belief that the act will result in the learning or NLO, about whether it is the most efficient way of teaching, and about the value of the results.

But the means-ends pattern allows us to rule out actions which the teacher does unconsciously, habits and mere mannerisms. The answer "Was I doing that?" rules out any attempt at taking a nervous arching of the eyebrows as that person's teaching. And the use of the pattern this way also rules out the attempt to make the mere movements of the teacher count as his teaching.[22]

Note, of course, that this does not preclude that "restrictions of manner" still hold on teaching claims: the claim that one is teaching, but using threats of force or lies, is open to falsification on the grounds that this sort of action cannot count as teaching even though it is done in order to get the students to learn. The pattern does not answer *everything;* just something.[23] But even this something is not to be ignored.

VI. BEHAVIORISM IS NOT ENTAILED BY MEANS-ENDS REASONING

Let us make explicit one assumption that has been implicit in the foregoing discussion: To use the means-ends pattern of reasoning does not commit one to using a behavioristic analysis of teaching or of its objectives.

Israel Scheffler has ably argued the case against behavioristic analysis of teaching, but his case depends in part upon viewing teaching as "aimed at getting someone to learn something."[24] One need not limit himself to this view in order to accept Scheffler's main point that no particular behavior is either necessary or sufficient evidence for the truth of the claim that one person is teaching something to another.

But another school of analysis has held that the objectives of teaching should be stated "behaviorally"; this directive is expressed in slogans such as "Stamp out non-behavioral objectives" and "Use behavioral objectives." But the attempt to make clear what these slogans mean has been unsuccessful. The most extensive development of the notion of behavior objectives (BO) is found in Robert F. Mager's *Preparing Objectives for Programmed Instruction.*[25] This text will

---

[22] Scheffler covers this problem in a different way by taking the teacher's intent to be the crucial question. *Op cit.,* pp. 64-67.

[23] Many of the further things to be considered under restrictions of manner and motive have been analyzed by B. Paul Komisar, who shows very ingeniously that a move by the teacher counts as a *teaching* move only if the students are aware of the intention to bring about some mental act on their part and can respond both to the move and to the intention with which it is performed. Cf. Komisar, "Teaching: Act and Enterprise," *Middle Atlantic States Philosophy of Education Society* (December, 1966). [See above, Ch. V. Editor's Note.]

[24] Scheffler, *op. cit.,* p. 68.

[25] Robert F. Mager, *Preparing Objectives for Programmed Instruction* (San Francisco: Fearon, 1961). Page references in parentheses in this section refer to this book.

serve here as whipping boy for our comments on the BO theory; other works might suffice, but this is widely used as a text and exemplifies both the strengths and weaknesses of this theory.

The BO theorists want most to avoid the teacher who says "I'm doing this in order that the students appreciate art (or understand physics, or know that $2 + 2 = 4$)" without being clear about what actions will serve as evidence of the student's having achieved the objective. Words such as 'know,' 'understand,' 'appreciate,' and 'believe' are "open to a wide range of interpretation" (p. 11), and are "not meaningful" in that they do not convey "to others a picture (of what a successful learner will be like) identical to the picture the writer has in mind." (p. 10)

But one is precluded from using these terms only as long as he does not specify what will count as the achievement of the objective:

> Though it is all right to include such words as "understand" and "appreciate" in a statement of an objective, the statement is not explicit enough to be useful until it indicates how you intend to sample the "understanding" and "appreciating." Until you describe what the learner will be *doing* when demonstrating that he "understands" or "appreciates", you have described very little at all. Thus, the statement which communicates best will be one which describes the terminal behavior of the learner well enough to preclude misinterpretation. (p. 11)

There is no particular problem with understanding Mager's point, although one might quibble with his terminology. But the BO doctrine goes on to specify what will count as achievement:

> A statement of an objective is useful to the extent that it specifies what the learner must be able to *do* or *perform* when he is demonstrating his mastery of the objective. (p. 13)

As an example, "To develop an appreciation for music" is rejected since it "neither precludes nor defines any behavior" (pp. 14-15), but "to be able to solve quadratic equations" is accepted since it "tells us what the learner will be doing when he is demonstrating that he has reached the goal." (pp. 14, 16) Other examples:

Acceptable: To be able to repair a radio. (pp. 18, 19)

Unacceptable: To know how an amplifier works. (pp. 18, 20)

Acceptable: To be able to write a summary of the factors leading to the depression of 1929. (pp. 19, 21)

Unacceptable: To understand the rules of logic. (pp. 19, 22)

To know the rules of football. (pp. 19, 23)

Each of the acceptable objectives, according to Mager, gives a description of the behavior of the student who has achieved the objective, while the others do not.

But the curious thing about the acceptable objectives is that they do not give descriptions of behavior, but rather specify criteria of correctness of *results* of behavior. A radio can be repaired by careful adjustment or (sometimes) by brute force. An equation may be solved by guess or by grind; the test of repairing or of solution is not in the behavior of the learner, but in the results of whatever he does do. Mager: "Now, repair the motor means to make it work. So *making it work* is the behavior desired." (p. 40) But, of course, there is no behavior that is in and of itself either necessary or sufficient evidence for concluding that a learner is making the motor (or radio, or equation) work.

The behavioral objectives, then, are not behavioral. The BO doctrine asks only that teachers specify what they are trying to achieve in rather precise terms. And of course, there is nothing wrong with this doctrine, when it is correctly described. The attempt to use means-ends reasoning in teaching requires some precision in the statement of the ends.

But there is another problem here. For the BO doctrine requires that the objectives be stated in terms of action; Mager thinks it necessary to add additional criteria of how well the learner performs. This takes two forms: (a) adding the redundant qualifier "correctly" ("The student must be able to correctly solve. . . ." p. 45) or specifying what counts as the correct solution ("The learner must be able to adjust the ion trap (of a TV receiver) to achieve a uniform raster . . ." p. 49); (b) specifying speeds, time limits, percentages of questions answered correctly, acceptable deviations from standards, or margins of allowable error. None of these is, strictly speaking, behavior or action. The danger is in the directive to use the language of action in developing educational objectives; the danger is that *only* "activity-goals" will be set, overlooking such important objectives as the way in which students go about doing whatever it is they are doing. 'Doing a dance gently' is not a behavioral objective, but a 'manner of acting' objective, if we may coin a phrase. (We suspect that most moral education involves something like this.) There is no way of translating 'gently' into a behavior or an action; there are empirical tests (i.e., ways of telling) for whether a person is being gentle or not, but they are not the same tests as one would use to tell if he were engaging in a given activitiy or behavior.

One can state the objectives of teaching in terms of future abilities, actions, manners of doing, and capacities, without committing the behavioristic fallacies of translating all of these into mere movement or even the softer fallacy of using only the language of action. Means-ends reasoning does not entail ruling out humanity.

VII. R. S. PETERS' APPARENT OBJECTIONS TO MEANS-ENDS REASONING IN EDUCATION ARE NOT OBJECTIONS

Among the more literate of modern critics of the use of means-ends reasoning in education is Professor R. S. Peters. His most concise criticism is found in the paper, "Must an Educator Have an Aim?", a chapter in *Authority, Responsibility and Education*.[26] In this paper, Peters argues that the means-ends pattern has been greatly over-used in education:

> For this model of adopting means to premeditated ends is one that haunts all our thinking about the promotion of what is valuable. In the educational sphere we therefore tend to look around for the equivalent of bridges to be built or ports to be steered to . . . . It is my conviction that this model misleads us in the sphere of education. We have got the wrong picture of the way in which values must enter into education; this is what occasions the disillusioned muttering about the absence of agreed aims. (p. 85)

One is sorely tempted to read this passage as if it said "means-ends reasoning has no place in the sphere of education." But this would be incorrect; for Peters' game here is not the "limited objective" of the teacher, like "getting at least six children through the eleven-plus," (p. 86) but rather, the "aims" in terms of which such objectives are often justified: mental health, self-realization, character, wisdom, and citizenship (his examples, pp. 86-87). In summarizing at the beginning of the next chapter, Peters says:

> I have admitted the importance of concrete and limited objectives but I have been very suspicious of over-all sounding aims like 'mental health' or 'self-development'. I have suggested that the crucial valuative questions, when we come down to moral brass tacks, are questions of principles and procedures. (p. 96)

---

[26] R. S. Peters, *Authority, Responsibility, and Education* (London: George Allen & Unwin, 1959). Page references in this section refer to this book. [See above, Ch. VI. Editor's Note.]

Now such a point is surely correct: the "aims" (if we want to stipulate a distinction here between aims and objectives) of education are clearly not something to be produced as one might produce plastic sailboats. But just as clearly, it is perfectly natural for the teacher to try to achieve *some* objective by teaching.

Peters' concern is important, and his objection to the view that value questions enter educational arguments *only* in the determination of objectives is quite correct. But from this it does not follow that arguments about what objectives (if any) our teachers and schools should achieve are empty of value content; nor does it follow that one can ignore empirical matters in deciding what procedures one should use in teaching. Value questions do enter into both "realms"; to ignore this fact is to miss the complexity of educational argument.

Peters does ignore questions about the nature of the logical relationship between the high-flown aims of education and the more limited objectives of the teacher's action. Peters views argument about aims as arguments about what sorts of procedures should be followed in education. But, if pressed, a teacher *might* justify his teaching by appeal to aims such as "good citizenship," "mental health," and so forth. So they are not necessarily arguments merely about procedures.

And here again, the means-ends pattern of reasoning may be of some use, even if only negatively. Let us consider yet another example. A history teacher is teaching about the development of the Bill of Rights of the American Constitution. Asked what he is doing, he answers, "I'm narrating the story of the development of the Bill of Rights to the class."

"Why?" (Assumption: He might be teaching about the personalities of the founding fathers, or the building of Independence Hall.)

"In order that the students later be able to recognize infringements of individual rights."

We may now ask (a) what evidence (rather, what kind of evidence) would support or contradict the teacher's claim to be doing what he says he's doing, (b) what further evidence is necessary to support or contradict his claim that he's doing so to produce a certain result, and (c) what evidence is necessary to support or contradict the claim that the end he was seeking has in fact been achieved.

a) If the teacher is speaking entirely in German and the students speak only French, this would count against his claim that he is narrating *to them* any story whatsoever. If, contrariwise, the students are obviously and keenly following the story, itself a complex activity,[27] this would presumably count as evidence for his claim. In neither case is the evidence conclusive. While speaking only German to mono-lingual French students, the teacher might convey *some* story just by gesture, rhythm, and style. And even when the students are following, it is not necessarily true that they are following the story the teacher claimed to be narrating. They might be following the bead of sweat on the teacher's nose. The point is this: In an actual teaching situa-tion we can usually decide rather quickly whether to give credence to the teacher's claim that he is doing X, where X is some logical cate-gory like narrating, describing, explaining, clarifying, etc. But when we come to give our grounds for accepting or rejecting his claim, we find that they are quite complex, involving convoluted relation-ships between what the teacher does and says and what the students do and say. (In turn the grounds for the truth of such claims overlap the criteria for deciding whether the teacher is doing *well* what he claims to be doing, but the grounds and criteria are not identical.)

b) Let us assume that we have satisfied ourselves that the teacher is narrating the story of the development of the Bill of Rights. But is it true that he is doing so in order that students will recognize in-fringements of individual rights in later life? What kind of evidence would count for or against that claim? (We take it to be no longer interesting to argue that such claims report some private mental state of the teacher.) Imagine a teacher who narrated the background of the Bill of Rights from a purely psychological or interpersonal per-spective, ignoring the questions of jurisprudence and politics involved. Imagine further that in that teacher's class a student should just hap-pen to mention a contemporary parallel to the kind of case the amend-ments were supposed to apply, whereupon the imaginary teacher says: "Shut up. I'm trying to tell you how Jefferson really felt about Frank-lin." The teacher's claim to be teaching in order to produce a capacity to recognize infringements would be highly dubious. If the details of our imaginary case are just reversed, we would take it as corroboration for the claim.

But not conclusive corroboration. The only way that we could for-mulate a statement of the teacher's actions that would decisively con-firm the hypothesis that he's teaching for a certain result is to formu-

---

[27] W. B. Gallie, *Philosophy and the Historical Understanding* (London: Chatto and Windus, 1964).

late a tautology: He is narrating the story of the development of the Bill of Rights in the manner one would use if he wanted students to learn from the story to recognize infringements of those rights in their own lives. And that is what gives us the trouble.

c) When we turn to the question of what evidence would constitute justification for the claim that the teaching was successful in achieving the end sought, we again have to formulate a tautology if the evidence is to be taken as decisive. It is easy enough to describe a case in which an ex-student was blatantly insensitive to infringements of individual rights, his own and those of others around him. But is even this conclusive? Not unless those infringements were of the sort that one should learn to recognize from a narrative account of the development of the Bill of Rights. Likewise for an ex-student who is zealous in precisely the proper degree in his recognition of infringements of rights. For 'zealous in precisely the proper degree' must be defined by reference to an intelligent and well-meaning man who has understood a narrative account of the development of the Bill of Rights.

The upshot is this: There are certain ways in which the claim that one is teaching for a certain end, call that C-1, is *formally* related to the claim that one has achieved a certain end *through teaching or by means of teaching* (call that C-2). Now if these claims are formally, not merely contingently, related, the means-ends pattern as defined above does not fit. But this can only be shown when the principles have been made explicit and the logical relationships between the teacher's limited objectives and the "high sounding aims" are clearer, for such things as "good citizenship" and "mental health" are defined partially as abilities like recognizing infringements of individual rights.

VIII. TEACHING MAY BE IMMORAL, BUT MEANS-ENDS REASONING DOES NOT MAKE IT SO

We anticipate a certain impatience in those readers who have come thus far in the essay. We have shown a clear parallel between the formal properties of paradigmatic means-ends reasoning on one hand, and the most natural way of describing-explaining-justifying teaching on the other. We have shown that reasoning about teaching cannot be captured in restrictive versions of the pattern, such as task-achievement analysis, or behaviorism, or Petersism; for the means-ends continuum that begins with the most minute teaching act *may* extend indefinitely toward the grandest goals Man can envision—just so long as the continuum includes some corresponding mental act by the person to whom the teaching is addressed. In short we have shown—sometimes conclusively, sometimes not—that the common conceptual objections to the use of means-ends reasoning about teaching simply do not hold.

But the impatient reader never believed much in those conceptual objections anyway. Oh, he might argue against the pattern conceptually, but his real antipathy goes deeper than concepts. Responding to the profound, disgusting, intolerable immorality of many, perhaps most, institutions of schooling, he is struck by the similarity of these institutions to manufacturing or agricultural enterprises where means-ends thinking is standard. Thus the impatient reader is likely to believe that we have missed the significant point: of course one can treat teaching as means to some end, but to do so is immoral, for it reduces teaching to the level of a non-human, mechanical (therefore inhumane) transaction.[28]

This kind of talk has three levels: puerile, prudential, and puzzling. It is puerile to argue, say, that because military commanders commonly employ means-ends reasoning in planning their barbarous atrocities, a teacher who uses means-ends reasoning in planning a lesson is planning a barbarous atrocity. Of course the teacher may conduct an atrocious lesson after planning, but we would ordinarily consider that a 'mis-use' rather than a necessary consequence of means-ends reasoning. In sum, we will grant that the paradigm cases of the pattern appear in the chain of human-action-followed-by-nonhuman-consequence, e.g., a tree's falling. But it is puerile to hold simply *on that account* that all uses of the pattern in thinking about a chain of human A's action—followed by human B's action—reduces (whatever that means) the latter to the former.

At the second, or prudential level, one encounters very good advice about how to better use (how not to 'mis-use') the means-ends pattern in teaching. In any concrete instance, an action-consequence relation is an abstraction from a much more complex situation containing all sorts of objects and events having all sorts of different relations. If

---

[28] See, for example, H. Millard Clements, "Introduction," *Moral Dilemmas of Schooling*, eds. H. Millard Clements and James B. Macdonald (Columbus, Ohio: Charles Merrill and Co., 1967); James B. Macdonald, "The Person in the Curriculum," and Dwayne Huebner, "Curriculum as a Field of Study," both in Helen F. Robison, ed., *Precedents and Promise in the Curriculum Field* (New York: Teachers College Press, 1966). [Huebner's paper is reprinted above, Ch. VII. Editor's note.]

reasoning about the total situation concentrates too exclusively on a particular action-consequence relation taken as means to ends, it may err in two different ways: (i) It may so concentrate on the desirable features of the chosen end that the undesirable aspects of the total situation are ignored. Thus many educators (for inscrutable reasons) believe that a child's learning to read is a worthwhile end; so worthwhile that it justifies not only certain teaching acts but also an institutional setting in which children are confined physically, constrained socially, and starved intellectually, (ii) It may so concentrate on an action's intended consequence that it ignores the longer term and unintended consequences of the same action. Thus we intend that our social studies teaching produce citizens who are loyal to the nation, but the longer run consequences include militarism and totalitarianism among large segments of the youth.

It is clearly prudential to avoid both those errors. Of course the end justifies the means, but no end justifies *any* means at all—only those means which are justifiable. (A child's learning to read justifies *teaching* him; not confining, constraining, and starving him.) Of course, one ought to consider the overall consequences of his actions, not just one consequence chosen as end. (What beside loyalty to country is learned when youth are taught to glorify our nation?) Such prudential considerations have been advanced by every system of substantive ethics which takes action serious. There is no novelty in excoriating linear thinking, if that means thinking about merely one line of action-consequence and ignoring all the rest that is happening in a situation and will happen as a result of what is done there.

But we submit that these prudential considerations do not preclude the use of means-ends reasoning; they rather establish the conditions for using it wisely. A teacher should be able to distinguish what he's doing to help the youngsters learn to read, e.g., teaching the ITA, flashing word object combinations on the board, from what else is happening in the same situation, e.g., children held passive, isolated, and protected from novel words and objects. Equally a teacher should be able to distinguish what he is teaching *for* from what all else will eventuate from a given situation. Is it good political therapy to tell a social studies teacher what he knows to be false, namely, that the *objective* of his teaching is militarism and Fascism? We doubt it. In sum, it is prudential to recognize and take account of the existential situation from which any actual means-ends reasoning is abstracted. But that is not to stop doing means-ends thinking.

But at a higher level still, there is a subtly puzzling feature about the pattern applied to teaching. You will recall that a value characterization is necessary for any outcome said to be the end for which an action is performed. If a teacher claims that what he's doing is done for X, then he must be prepared to argue either that X is good in itself or else that X leads, in turn, to some Y which . . . is good in itself. We have not argued directly that any time a person claims to be teaching he must be prepared to offer a means-ends description-explanation-justification of his action, but we argued that only actions intended to foster further mental acts in others would clearly count as teaching.

The difference between what we have and have not argued is this: Consider a person going through the standard moves a teacher makes, under usual conditions, etc. Suppose that person should convince us (a) that he would call what he is doing 'teaching' and (b) that he is utterly unaware of any intended end for his action. We have not argued nor would we, that the term 'teaching' is inapplicable to what he does. We might say "A madman teaches in that school," but that affirms teaching. But now suppose that we are required to observe that madman for the purpose of distinguishing those of his actions or movements which count as teaching from his extraneous, accidental, or erroneous movements. The only way, we have argued, for making that distinction is by appeal to the mental acts he intends to produce in the persons to whom the teaching is directed. We should have to say: This move counts as teaching, because we could imagine its being made by a person who did intend to induce an appropriate mental act . . . etc.

But now the puzzling part: Mental acts are just the sorts of things which are either justifiable in themselves without appeal to further consequences or else are not justifiable at all. *One person's thinking, willing, feeling, understanding, believing, opining . . . cannot legitimately be another person's means to some further end.* To violate that canon is to violate the Kantian imperative that men are to be treated as ends and not as means. One can well argue whether, say, a given thought is one a child should have. It is good for a child (or anyone else, for that matter) to think generously rather than selfishly, magnanimously rather than vindictively, etc. But that child's generous thoughts ought not be the teacher's or school's or society's means to something else. Thus the means-ends pattern that seems, in paradigmatic cases like tree-felling, to be infinite in scope, when used to talk about teaching, seems to stop after the first exchange. There . . . undoubtedly are further consequences of children's having true beliefs instead of false, good will instead of hatred, kindly feelings instead of hostile, well grounded opinions instead of prejudices. But it is not to bring about those further consequences—whatever they may be—that we teach. Our only justifiable end is that children have true beliefs, good will, etc., rather than the opposites.

When children's mental acts are used by adults as means to further ends, for instance, to enhance the power of political or economic systems, we can join the opponents of the means-ends pattern in declaiming against manipulation and exploitation. But let us be clear that it is these ends we are against, not the means-ends pattern itself. It is only when 'learning' is taken as the implied end of teaching that the exploitative, manipulative use of means-ends thinking seems to occur. But that's another story, another essay.

INDEX

151